Property and Liability Risk Control

Property and Liability Risk Control

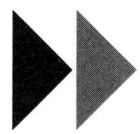

Second Edition • First Printing

American Institute for Chartered Property Casualty
Underwriters/Insurance Institute of America
720 Providence Road, Suite 100
Malvern, Pennsylvania 19355-3433

© 2008
American Institute for Chartered Property Casualty Underwriters/Insurance Institute of America

All rights reserved. This book or any part thereof may not be reproduced without the written permission of the copyright holder.

Unless otherwise apparent, examples used in AICPCU/IIA materials related to this course are based on hypothetical situations and are for educational purposes only. The characters, persons, products, services, and organizations described in these examples are fictional. Any similarity or resemblance to any other character, person, product, services, or organization is merely coincidental. AICPCU/IIA is not responsible for such coincidental or accidental resemblances.

This material may contain Internet Web site links external to AICPCU/IIA. AICPCU/IIA neither approves nor endorses any information, products, or services to which any external Web sites refer. Nor does AICPCU/IIA control these Web sites' content or the procedures for Web site content development.

AICPCU/IIA specifically disclaims any implied warranties of merchantability or fitness for a particular purpose. No warranty may be created or extended by sales representatives or written sales materials.

AICPCU/IIA materials related to this course are provided with the understanding that AICPCU/IIA is not engaged in rendering legal, accounting, or other professional service. Nor is AICPCU/IIA explicitly or implicitly stating that any of the processes, procedures, or policies described in the materials are the only appropriate ones to use. The advice and strategies contained herein may not be suitable for every situation.

Information which is copyrighted by and proprietary to Insurance Services Office, Inc. ("ISO Material") is included in this publication. Use of the ISO Material is limited to ISO Participating Insurers and their Authorized Representatives. Use by ISO Participating Insurers is limited to use in those jurisdictions for which the insurer has an appropriate participation with ISO. Use of the ISO Material by Authorized Representatives is limited to use solely on behalf of one or more ISO Participating Insurers.

Second Edition • First Printing • August 2008

Library of Congress Control Number: 2008931746

ISBN 978-0-89463-377-5

Foreword

The American Institute for Chartered Property Casualty Underwriters and the Insurance Institute of America (the Institutes) are independent, not-for-profit organizations committed to expanding the knowledge of professionals in risk management, insurance, financial services, and related fields through education and research.

In accordance with our belief that professionalism is grounded in education, experience, and ethical behavior, the Institutes provide a wide range of educational programs designed to meet the needs of individuals working in risk management and property-casualty insurance The American Institute offers the Chartered Property Casualty Underwriter (CPCU®) professional designation, designed to provide a broad understanding of the property-casualty insurance industry. CPCU students may select either a commercial or a personal risk management and insurance focus, depending on their professional needs.

The Insurance Institute of America (IIA) offers designations and certificate programs in a variety of disciplines, including the following:

- Claims
- Commercial underwriting
- Fidelity and surety bonding
- General insurance
- Insurance accounting and finance
- Insurance information technology
- Insurance production and agency management
- Insurance regulation and compliance
- Management
- Marine insurance
- Personal insurance
- Premium auditing
- Quality insurance services
- Reinsurance
- Risk management
- Surplus lines

You may choose to take a single course to fill a knowledge gap, complete a program leading to a designation, or take multiple courses and programs throughout your career. No matter which approach you choose, you will gain practical knowledge and skills that will contribute to your professional growth and enhance your education and qualifications in the expanding insurance market. In addition, many CPCU and IIA courses qualify for credits toward certain associate, bachelor's, and master's degrees at several prestigious colleges and universities, and all CPCU and IIA courses carry college credit recommendations from the American Council on Education.

The American Institute for CPCU was founded in 1942 through a collaborative effort between industry professionals and academics, led by faculty members at The Wharton School of the University of Pennsylvania. In 1953, the American Institute for CPCU merged with the Insurance Institute of America, which was founded in 1909 and which remains the oldest continuously functioning national organization offering educational programs for the property-casualty insurance business.

The Insurance Research Council (IRC), founded in 1977, helps the Institutes fulfill the research aspect of their mission. A division of the Institutes, the IRC is supported by industry members. This not-for-profit research organization examines public policy issues of interest to property-casualty insurers, insurance customers, and the general public. IRC research reports are distributed widely to insurance-related organizations, public policy authorities, and the media.

The Institutes strive to provide current, relevant educational programs in formats and delivery methods that meet the needs of insurance professionals and the organizations that employ them. Institute textbooks are an essential component of the education we provide. Each book is designed to clearly and concisely provide the practical knowledge and skills you need to enhance your job performance and career. The content is developed by the Institutes in collaboration with risk management and insurance professionals and members of the academic community. We welcome comments from our students and course leaders; your feedback helps us continue to improve the quality of our study materials.

Peter L. Miller, CPCU
President and CEO
American Institute for CPCU
Insurance Institute of America

Preface

This is the second of two texts used in CPCU 557, the Survey of Commercial Risk Management and Insurance. The other text for CPCU 557, *Commercial Insurance*, examines the major lines of commercial insurance in a risk management context. Both insurance and risk control are key tools in any risk management program. To achieve a more complete discussion of risk management, this text examines the risk control aspect. Chapter 1 covers property risk control, and Chapter 2 covers liability risk control.

Chapter 1 describes the elements of fire loss; measures for pre-loss fire control; systems, devices, and resources used for internal and external protection against hostile fires; measures for controlling water damage from firefighting efforts or from sprinkler leakage; and measures for preventing or reducing losses caused by theft, explosion, windstorm, flood, and earthquake.

Chapter 2 discusses major types of risk control techniques for liability loss exposures and how organizations can use those techniques to control loss events and manage claims. The chapter examines how organizations can control the following loss exposures: premises and operations liability, products liability, automobile liability, and workers compensation and employers liability.

The material in this book is extracted from the textbooks for CPCU 551 (*Commercial Property Risk Management and Insurance*) and CPCU 552 (*Commercial Liability Risk Management and Insurance*). Many authors and reviewers have contributed to these chapters and refined them over the years, and they are acknowledged in the CPCU 551 and CPCU 552 textbooks.

For more information about the Institutes' programs, please call our Customer Service Department at (800) 644-2101, e-mail us at customerservice@cpcuiia.org, or visit our Web site at www.aicpcu.org.

American Institute for CPCU
Insurance Institute of America

Contents

Chapter 1
Property Risk Control	1.1
Risk Control for Fire Losses	1.5
Risk Control for Theft Losses	1.33
Risk Control for Other Causes of Loss	1.40
Summary	1.43

Chapter 2
Liability Risk Control	2.1
Risk Control Techniques	2.3
General Concepts of Commercial Liability Risk Control	2.5
Controlling Premises and Operations Liability Losses	2.9
Controlling Products Liability Losses	2.12
Controlling Automobile Liability Losses	2.18
Controlling Workers Compensation and Employers Liability Losses	2.20
Summary	2.28
Index	1

Direct Your Learning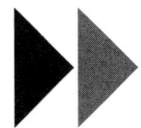

Property Risk Control

Educational Objectives

After learning the content of this chapter and completing the corresponding course guide assignment, you should be able to:

▶ Describe the elements of fire and their significance in fire risk control.

▶ Describe the different types of building construction according to the definitions of Insurance Services Office, Inc., and how the construction types differ in resisting fire.

▶ Describe various pre-loss fire control measures.

▶ Describe the internal and external facilities that can be used to detect and extinguish fires, including measures for controlling water damage and other losses resulting from a fire.

▶ Describe risk control measures for losses caused by the following types of theft:
- Burglary
- Robbery
- Employee theft

▶ Describe risk control measures for losses caused by the following:
- Explosion
- Windstorm
- Flood
- Earthquake

▶ Recommend appropriate property risk control measures for a described organization.

OUTLINE

Risk Control for Fire Losses

Risk Control for Theft Losses

Risk Control for Other Causes of Loss

Summary

 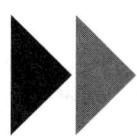

Chapter 1: Develop Your Perspective

What are the main topics covered in the chapter?

Chapter 1 examines the risk control measures that an organization can use to prevent or reduce property losses caused by fire, theft, and some other important causes of property loss.

Examine the building in which you work.

- What type of construction does the building have, and how does this type of construction affect the building's susceptibility to fire damage?
- Does your building have a sprinkler system, standpipes, or fire extinguishers?

Why is it important to learn about these topics?

By recognizing and recommending appropriate risk control measures, you can help an insured organization to prevent property losses and to keep insurance costs down.

Consider a museum director who refuses to install a sprinkler system because he or she believes that the potential for water damage is greater than the potential for fire.

- Is the museum director's argument valid?
- How might you approach the director about this issue? What recommendations would you make?

How can you use what you will learn?

Review a survey report prepared by an insurer's loss control representative after inspecting a policyholder's building.

- What are the technical terms the loss control representative uses regarding property loss exposures? Do you understand what these terms mean?
- If you were the loss control representative, what risk control recommendations would you make to the occupant of the building based on your report?

Property Risk Control

Every organization is exposed to the possibility of accidental loss. Regardless of whether an organization is a business enterprise or a charitable institution, accidental loss can keep the organization from achieving its objectives or can even bankrupt it. Accordingly, most organizations seek to manage their loss exposures by preventing accidents, by taking measures to reduce the size of losses that occur, and by using insurance or some other method to pay for losses that cannot be prevented or reduced.

An organization's loss exposures can be categorized as property loss exposures, liability loss exposures, personnel loss exposures, and net income loss exposures, as defined in Exhibit 1-1. All of these loss exposures can be handled by applying the risk management process, shown in Exhibit 1-2. Application of the risk management process results in the implementation of appropriate risk management techniques. All risk management techniques can be classified as either risk control or risk financing. Risk control techniques are intended to avoid loss exposures or to reduce their frequency and/or severity. Risk financing techniques are intended to pay for losses that occur. Exhibit 1-3 summarizes specific risk control techniques and risk financing techniques.

This text focuses on the use of risk control to handle commercial property, net income, and liability loss exposures. The present chapter examines risk control techniques for some of the most important causes of property and net income loss: fire, theft, explosion, windstorm, flood, and earthquake. Chapter 2 examines risk control techniques for major commercial liability loss exposures.

EXHIBIT 1-1

Loss Exposure Definitions

Property loss exposure: A condition that presents the possibility that a person or an organization will sustain a loss resulting from damage (including destruction, taking, or loss of use) to property in which that person or organization has a financial interest.

Liability loss exposure: A condition that presents the possibility that a person or an organization will sustain a loss resulting from a claim made against that person or organization by someone seeking money damages or some other legal remedy.

Personnel loss exposure: A condition that presents the possibility of loss caused by a key person's death, disability, retirement, or resignation that deprives an organization of that person's special skill or knowledge that the organization cannot readily replace.

Net income loss exposure: A condition that presents the possibility of loss caused by a reduction in net income.

EXHIBIT 1-2
The Risk Management Process

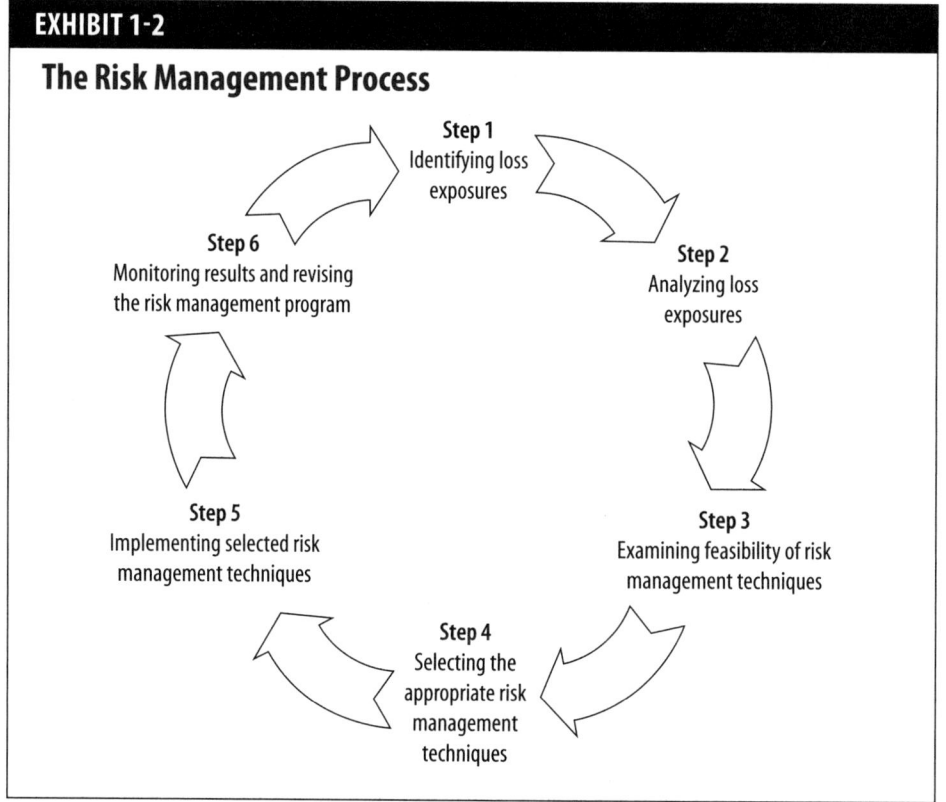

EXHIBIT 1-3
Risk Management Techniques

Summary of Risk Control Techniques

Avoidance eliminates any possibility of loss. The probability of loss from an avoided loss exposure is zero because an entity decides not to assume a loss exposure in the first place (proactive avoidance) or to eliminate one that already exists (abandonment).

Loss prevention involves reducing the frequency of a particular loss.

Loss reduction involves reducing the severity of a particular loss.

Separation involves dispersing a particular activity or asset over several locations. Separation involves the routine, daily reliance on each of the separated assets or activities, all of which regularly form a portion of the organization's working resources.

Duplication involves relying on backups, that is, spares or duplicates, used only if primary assets or activities suffer loss.

Diversification involves providing a range of products and services used by a variety of customers.

Summary of Risk Financing Techniques

Retention involves generating funds from within the organization to pay for losses.

Transfer involves generating funds from outside the organization to pay for losses and includes insurance and noninsurance transfer.

In applying the risk management process, one should always consider risk control, even when losses are financed by insurance. Effective risk control serves to reduce both expected losses and the cost of financing losses. Moreover, because some loss costs are not covered by insurance (such as expenses to recover market position), risk control can reduce risk financing costs even when an organization has full insurance. In addition to their monetary benefits, risk control measures can reduce uncertainty and help the organization meet its risk management objectives. Even if they do not directly reduce the organization's insurance premiums, risk control measures are likely to make getting and keeping insurance easier for the organization.

RISK CONTROL FOR FIRE LOSSES

Fire losses, like most other losses, result from chains of events. The 1967 McCormick Place fire in Chicago illustrates a sequence of events that led to a major loss. McCormick Place was an exhibition center that opened in 1960. When the fire occurred, the facility contained an exhibition consisting of 1,250 exhibits constructed of highly flammable materials.

The loss and its severity resulted from a conjunction of unrelated things that went wrong. In the McCormick Place exhibition hall, the exhibitors' need for electrical outlets had not been anticipated. Available circuits were overloaded with extension cords. One exhibitor used a defective cord that ran among other exhibits made of light, combustible materials such as cardboard, light-pressed panels, and paper. Because the combustibility of contents in the exhibits had not been specifically considered during the building's design phase (despite the building's intended use) and the ceiling was extremely high, the exhibition area was not sprinklered.

A fire began while the hall was unoccupied. The blaze had grown substantially before a guard saw it, and it took three or four minutes for him to reach an alarm station. When firefighters arrived, they found that valves on the lines to the fire hydrants had been left partially closed, seriously reducing dynamic water pressure. The firefighters did not know where the valves were. This series of events resulted in catastrophic fire damage and one death. Many unsafe acts and physical hazards combined to produce this result. For example, the valve problem with the hydrants was itself caused by a chain of events.

Risk control measures are designed to deal with links in the chain of events leading to loss. The use of specific risk control measures depends on the nature of the particular perils and hazards being addressed. As used in this text, the word "peril" is synonymous with cause of loss, and the word "hazard" refers to a condition that increases the frequency and/or severity of loss.

Generally, risk control measures take one or both of two approaches. The engineering approach attacks hazards by reviewing and improving the design and location of properties and equipment, to reduce the number of hazards. The human behavior approach attacks hazards by modifying people's behavior to reduce the frequency of unsafe acts. Although losses are usually caused by unsafe acts (note the several human failures in the exhibition hall loss chain), engineering often can be used to exclude or limit the opportunities for unsafe acts to be committed in the first place and to limit the losses that may result from unsafe acts. For example, automatic sprinklers can successfully interrupt fire loss chains that people have started, and fences and locked gates can keep people from tampering with equipment.

Elements of Fire

Breaking a chain of loss-causing events requires knowledge of how the events proceed—how one thing leads to another. Three elements are required to have a fire in the smoldering stage: an initial source of heat, oxygen, and fuel. A fourth ingredient—an uninterrupted chemical chain reaction—is required to support a flaming (as opposed to a smoldering) fire. As more fuel burns, the amount of heat present usually increases. Strong fires create their own air drafts, bringing more oxygen to the fuel and allowing the fire to grow by engulfing more fuel.

Most fire loss prevention and reduction efforts therefore center on removing one or more of the three basic elements of fire: heat, oxygen, and fuel.

Heat

Four types of energy can create heat sufficient to cause a fire: electrical heat energy, chemical heat energy, mechanical (frictional) heat energy, and nuclear heat energy.

- *Electrical heat energy* may come from natural sources (such as lightning) or artificial ones (such as power-generating plants). It may be dynamic (for example, power flowing through power lines and operating motors) or static (such as the charge in a storage battery).
- *Chemical heat energy* is released as part of a chemical reaction. Examples include the burning of a welding torch and the spontaneous combustion of oily rags left in a closet.
- *Mechanical, or frictional, heat energy* is developed when objects rub together. The brakes on a car create heat, as does the friction of a grinding wheel on a piece of metal, or a defective bearing.
- *Nuclear heat energy* is released by nuclear fission or fusion. Controlled nuclear reaction creates a source of heat that is converted to electricity in nuclear power plants. Uncontrolled release in a nuclear accident, or the controlled or uncontrolled release of a nuclear weapon, can cause widespread damage from both heat and ionizing radiation.

What is commonly called *solar energy* is not a separate type of heat energy but, rather, is nuclear heat energy (also known as radiant heat) transmitted to Earth by electromagnetic waves. Solar energy can heat materials such as the collectors in a solar heating system, or it can be converted to electricity. If sufficiently concentrated (as when sun rays are refracted through a lens), solar energy can create temperatures sufficient for a fire.

It is important to identify all the heat sources from which fire damage might arise in order to give each of them proper risk control treatment. The specifics of treatment differ according to whether the source is planned or unplanned, fixed or mobile.

Some heat sources are deliberately installed because they are needed for the organization's operations: these can be called "planned" sources. Others are present or brought in without the intention of the organization's management: they may be called "unplanned" sources.

Standard examples of planned sources include a wide variety of heat-creating equipment, ranging from soldering irons to blast furnaces. Heating furnaces, boilers, and welding and cutting torches are planned heat sources.

Unplanned heat sources consist primarily of those that management has not been able, or has not tried, to control. Examples include smoking by employees and visitors, using personal heaters in a work area, and elements such as lightning that no amount of planning can eliminate.

Some heat sources are fixed, while others move around. Furnaces and boilers for heating buildings are fixed. Welding and cutting torches are common mobile sources of heat, as are forklift trucks and other vehicles.

Oxygen

Fire is a rapid oxidation process with the evolution of light and heat in varying intensities. Oxidation is a process that requires atmospheric oxygen or oxygen liberated from an oxygen-containing compound. Most fires obtain their necessary supply from ordinary air, about 21 percent of which is oxygen. Without sufficient oxygen, fires die (are smothered). A hot fire tends to develop its own air supply by creating a draft: air heated by the fire rises in a thermal column, leaving a low-pressure area below into which fresh air flows.

The more favorable the conditions for oxygen supply, the faster and hotter the fire burns, and when oxygen is abundant, fuels flame at lower temperatures. Consequently, oxygen-rich atmospheres (used in oxygen tents in hospitals, for example, and in some industrial processes) increase the probability of a fire.

A few substances can burn without an outside oxygen supply. All of these are self-oxidants (such as nitrous oxide and nitrocellulose). Their physical structure includes enough combined oxygen to support flame for a time. Some self-oxidizing compounds, like nitrate-based explosives, can detonate (undergo extremely rapid combustion with an associated supersonic shock wave). A few special chemical combinations can produce fire without any free oxygen.

Fuel

For a fire to start, continue, or spread, it must have fuel. Fuels vary greatly in the ease with which they can be ignited. Gasoline vapor is more ignitable than paper, paper more ignitable than framing lumber, framing lumber more ignitable than heavy timbers, and so on. The relative combustibility of a fuel depends on the amount of heat required to cause it to produce enough burnable vapors to mix with oxygen in the air and ignite. In a practical situation, two characteristics of a fuel are important: the temperature at which it vaporizes (a function of its chemical composition) and the extent to which it holds heat rather than spreads it (a matter strongly affected by the size and shape of the fuel, its density, and its chemistry).

Autoignition temperature
The lowest temperature to which a substance must be heated for it to ignite without a separate ignition source.

An important characteristic of any substance is its **autoignition temperature**, or kindling point. Autoignition temperature is the lowest temperature to which a substance must be heated for it to ignite without a separate ignition source. The autoignition temperature of paper, for example, is 451°F. A substance that has reached its autoignition temperature will continue to release sufficient vapors to burn and will continue to burn until all the fuel is consumed or the fire is extinguished.

Flash point
The lowest temperature at which a combustible liquid releases vapors that can be ignited by a spark or flame.

An important characteristic of any combustible liquid is its **flash point**. The flash point is the minimum temperature at which a combustible liquid (or solid) releases vapor sufficient to form an ignitable mixture with air near the surface of the liquid (or solid). Gasoline, for instance, has a flash point of -45°F, compared with diesel fuel's flash point of between 126°F and 204°F (the exact blend of petroleum distillates varies). At room temperature, gasoline releases enough vapors to mix with air and be readily ignited. Diesel fuel will not release sufficient vapors to ignite until it is heated to its flash point (126-204°F), so it is much less likely than gasoline to be the cause of a fire resulting from accidental ignition of vapors.

Wood in a toothpick and the same kind of wood in a dry log both have the same autoignition temperature. But, when the surface of a toothpick is heated, the heat has little place else to go, and the toothpick quickly ignites. In a log, however, some of the heat at the surface is dissipated into the interior. As a result, a hotter or longer-sustained heat supply is required to ignite the log. When external heat is removed, the cool interior of the log may absorb enough heat to bring the log's surface temperature below the autoignition temperature.

Continuing fire represents an ongoing reaction. When one starts a wood fire in a fireplace, initial heat may be created by friction (striking a match). The process continues as the chemicals in the match head burn, eventually setting the wood of the match aflame. The temperature thus created is not extremely high, but the shape and material of the match cause the fire to be a self-sustaining chain reaction. In the fireplace, the burning match ignites paper and light wood materials with autoignition temperatures below the temperature produced by the match's flame. More fuel catches fire, generating even more heat. If the temperature is high enough and is sustained long enough, the logs can be induced to flame because the fire from already burning materials applies heat more rapidly than it can be dissipated into the air and into the logs' interior. Eventually, if enough heat is produced rapidly enough, logs can continue to burn on their own, without any continuing outside source of heat.

The process is the same with most hostile fires. (A hostile fire is one that burns outside of any receptacle normally intended for containing fires, such as a furnace or stove.) In severe cases, the buildup of heat increases so rapidly as more and more fuel reaches its autoignition temperature, that the fire cannot be stopped until it has completely consumed all available fuel. The fuel for most hostile fires consists of buildings and their contents.

The variety of building contents that may be exposed to fire is tremendous. For example, depending on a building's type of operations and its particular location, inventory may be paper or pig iron, alcohol or asbestos, sulfur or silicon. Equipment and furnishings may be readily combustible or almost noncombustible, oily or clean, light or heavy. Not only the inherent flammability of each type of building contents, but also its spacing and arrangement determine its significance as fuel for fire. Each occupancy, and in many cases each part of a single occupancy, presents a different exposure.

The expected amount of combustibles available as fuel for a hostile fire in a given area is called the **fire load**, commonly expressed in terms of weight of combustibles per square foot. Heat to be expected in a fire is estimated on the basis of known calorific content of those combustibles present in a building's contents and structural components. (The "calorific content" of anything is the amount of heat—number of calories—produced when it burns.) Because physical arrangement of the material greatly affects the amount of heat produced in any given amount of time, estimation of fire load in specific cases requires expert judgment.

Fire load
The expected amount of combustibles available as fuel for a hostile fire in a given area, commonly expressed in terms of weight of combustibles per square foot.

Most high fire loads do not result from materials recognized as especially hazardous. Where possible, care is usually taken to limit the amount of such exposure in a building. Rather, common high load cases occur in bulk storage or relatively low-hazard materials packed together in great quantity in a minimum of space. Modern lifting equipment allows stacking to considerable heights, which can create extreme fire loads. The very heaviest fire loads, however, occur in situations with large quantities of extraordinarily hazardous materials. Such materials include highly flammable liquids (such as light petroleum products, lacquers, or alcohols) and materials that burn explosively, or nearly so (such as sulfur and some sulfides, many nitrates, some peroxides, and many types of metallic or organic dusts).

A fire load includes the combustible parts of a building. Wooden buildings, of course, contribute more ready fuel for fire than do buildings of masonry, noncombustible, or fire-resistive materials. When building materials are combustible, the common result is more damage to the building itself and faster spread of the fire to other fuel inside or outside the building. Because of the importance of building construction to fire risk control and fire insurance rating, knowing how well different types of building construction resist fire is helpful.

Types of Building Construction

This discussion is based on the construction definitions used by Insurance Services Office, Inc. (ISO) in determining property insurance premiums. The National Fire Protection Association (NFPA), various building codes, appraisal guides, and some insurance publications use classifications different from those used by ISO. In each case, construction types are categorized according to the needs of those using the system. Any of these building classification systems can be useful in evaluating fire loss exposures and developing appropriate alternatives for controlling fire losses.

Frame Construction

In **frame construction** (ISO Code 1), a building's exterior walls are constructed of wood or other combustible materials, even if combined with other materials such as brick or stucco. Thus, a building with a single thickness of brick (brick veneer) supported by wood framing is considered a frame building. Many dwellings and small mercantile buildings are of frame construction. The popularity of frame construction varies considerably by geographic region. The combustibility of wood makes frame buildings susceptible to fire damage; because everything is held up by wood, a fire can destroy the structure, or the involved part of it. Exhibit 1-4 illustrates frame construction.

Joisted Masonry Construction

In **joisted masonry construction** (ISO Code 2), the exterior walls are made of masonry materials such as brick, stone, concrete, or even adobe, and these walls do not depend on wood or other combustible materials for support. Other supporting elements of the building, such as the joists and beams that support the roof and floors, are made of wood. The roof and floors themselves are also usually made of wood or other combustible materials. Exhibits 1-5 and 1-6 illustrate joisted masonry construction.

> **Frame construction**
> A type of construction in which the exterior walls of the building are constructed of wood or other combustible materials, even if combined with other materials such as brick or stucco.
>
> **Joisted masonry construction**
> A type of construction in which the exterior walls are made of masonry materials such as brick, stone, or concrete, and these walls do not depend on wood or other combustible materials for support; other supporting elements, such as the joists and beams, are made of wood.

EXHIBIT 1-4

Frame Construction

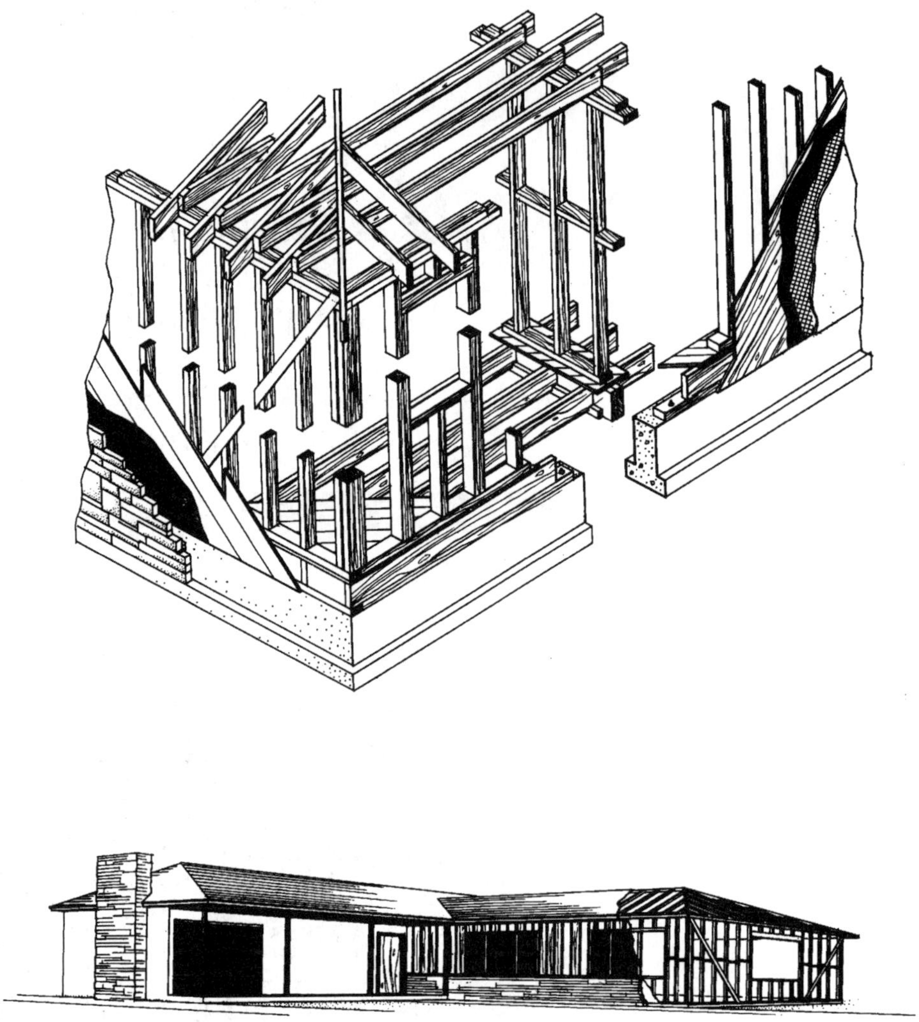

Reprinted with permission from *Stevens Valuation Quarterly* (Los Angeles: Marshall and Swift Publication Company, July 1973), p. A-12.

EXHIBIT 1-5

Joisted Masonry Construction

Reprinted with permission from *Stevens Valuation Quarterly* (Los Angeles: Marshall and Swift Publication Company, July 1973), p. A-11.

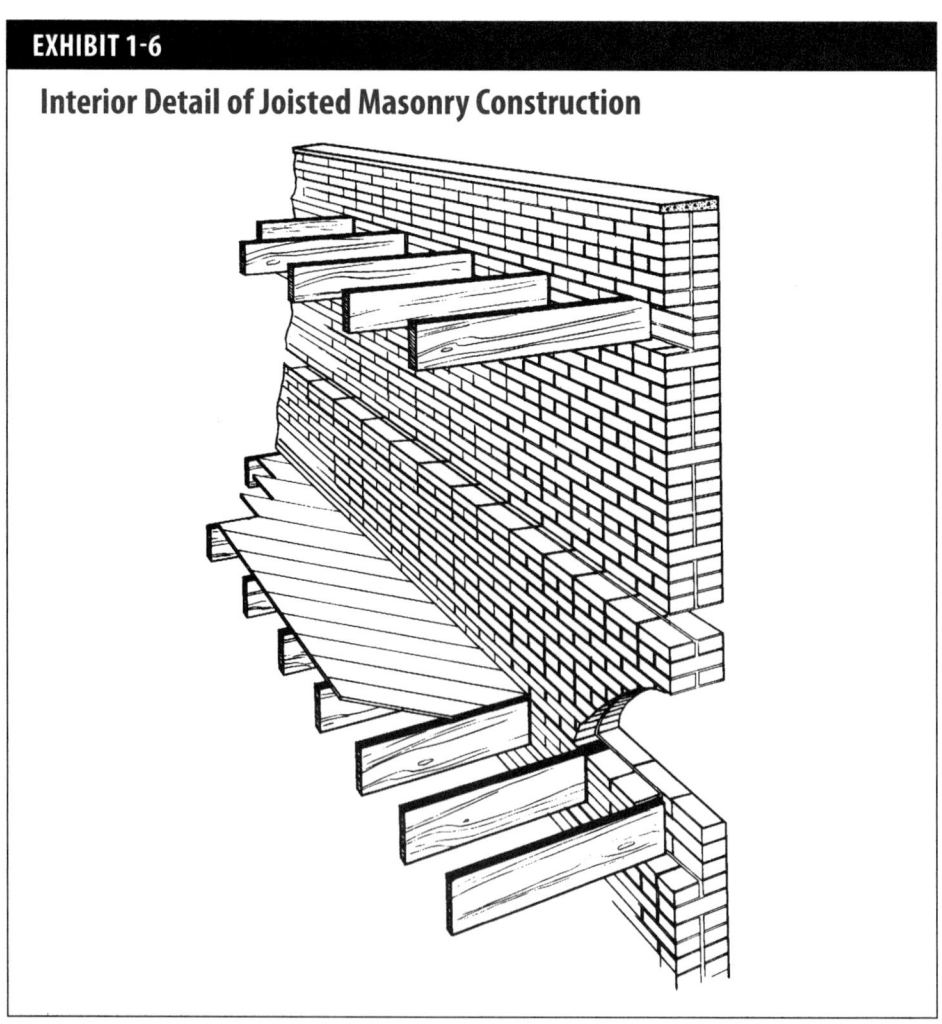

EXHIBIT 1-6

Interior Detail of Joisted Masonry Construction

Reprinted with permission from *Stevens Valuation Quarterly* (Los Angeles: Marshall and Swift Publication Company, July 1973), p. A-11.

When a joisted masonry building suffers an intense fire, only a shell will be left—the bare exterior walls. A significant portion of the walls may even fall or be pulled or pushed down by collapse of the roof or wooden support beams. If the building has brick walls, the bricks themselves can be damaged beyond use by prolonged exposure to intense heat. In less-intense fires, the exterior bearing walls usually remain in usable, or nearly usable, condition; they continue to support the roof, and the walls and roof provide some degree of protection for the interior. Joisted masonry construction is usually preferable to frame construction when fire occurs.

A type of joisted masonry construction called **heavy timber**, or **mill construction**, is considered more fire resistant than typical joisted masonry construction. Used mainly in older industrial buildings, heavy timber construction involves heavy timber structural supports and masonry wall construction. Large, solid pieces of wood are extremely difficult to burn. Thus, a bare wooden beam eight inches by ten inches in diameter ordinarily resists fire damage better than a bare steel beam with the same load-bearing capacity. Although the steel beam will not burn, it will warp and twist in a large fire and lose its strength.

> **Heavy timber construction (mill construction)**
> A type of joisted masonry construction that is considered more fire resistant than typical joisted masonry construction.

Noncombustible Construction

Noncombustible construction (ISO Code 3) is a specialized term in fire protection and fire insurance. The term is *not* applied to all buildings of noncombustible materials—many such buildings fall into the fire-resistive category. A building is in the noncombustible class when its exterior walls, floors, and roof are constructed of, and supported by, metal, gypsum, or other noncombustible materials that will contribute little, if any, fuel to a fire.

One common type of noncombustible construction, illustrated in Exhibit 1-7, is all-metal construction—light metal walls and roof, with light metal supports.

> **Noncombustible construction**
> A type of construction in which the exterior walls, floor, and roof of a building are constructed of, and supported by, metal, gypsum, or other noncombustible materials.

EXHIBIT 1-7

Light Noncombustible Construction

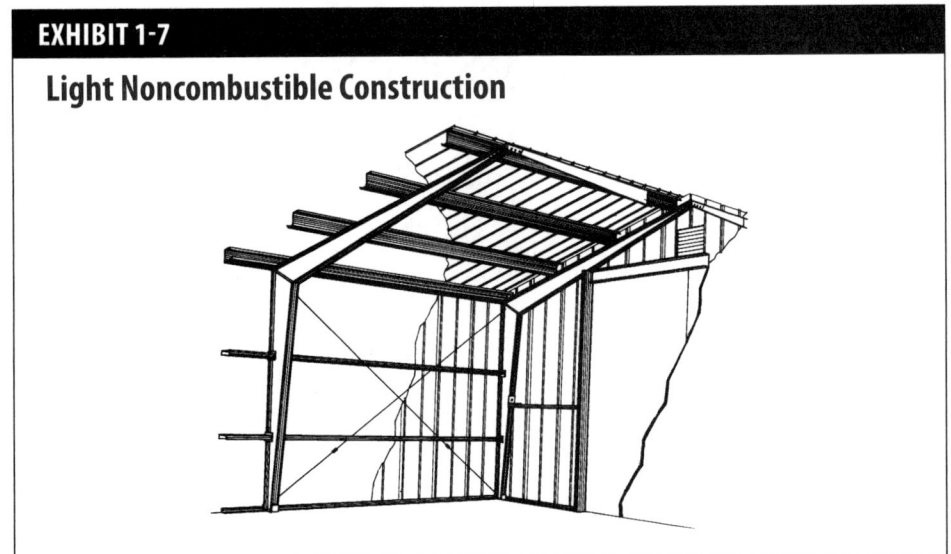

Reprinted with permission from *Stevens Valuation Quarterly* (Los Angeles: Marshall and Swift Publication Company, July 1973), p. A-11.

Many light noncombustible buildings do not add fuel to fires but are susceptible to heat damage from fires involving building contents. Exposed to fire, their structural members expand, twist, crack, and otherwise deteriorate, often resulting in collapse and total loss of the building, increased damage to contents, and increased threat to life safety. Despite their metal components, noncombustible buildings are not necessarily safer than buildings of frame or joisted masonry construction.

Masonry Noncombustible Construction

In **masonry noncombustible construction** (ISO Class 4), a building's exterior walls are made of masonry materials, and the floors and roof are made of metal or some other noncombustible material. Masonry noncombustible buildings are generally more resistant to fire damage than any of the preceding types. Exhibit 1-8 illustrates a portion of a wall and the adjoining metal roof joists in a masonry noncombustible building.

> **Masonry noncombustible construction**
> A type of construction in which the exterior walls are made of masonry materials, and the floor and roof are made of metal or some other noncombustible material.

EXHIBIT 1-8

Masonry Noncombustible Construction

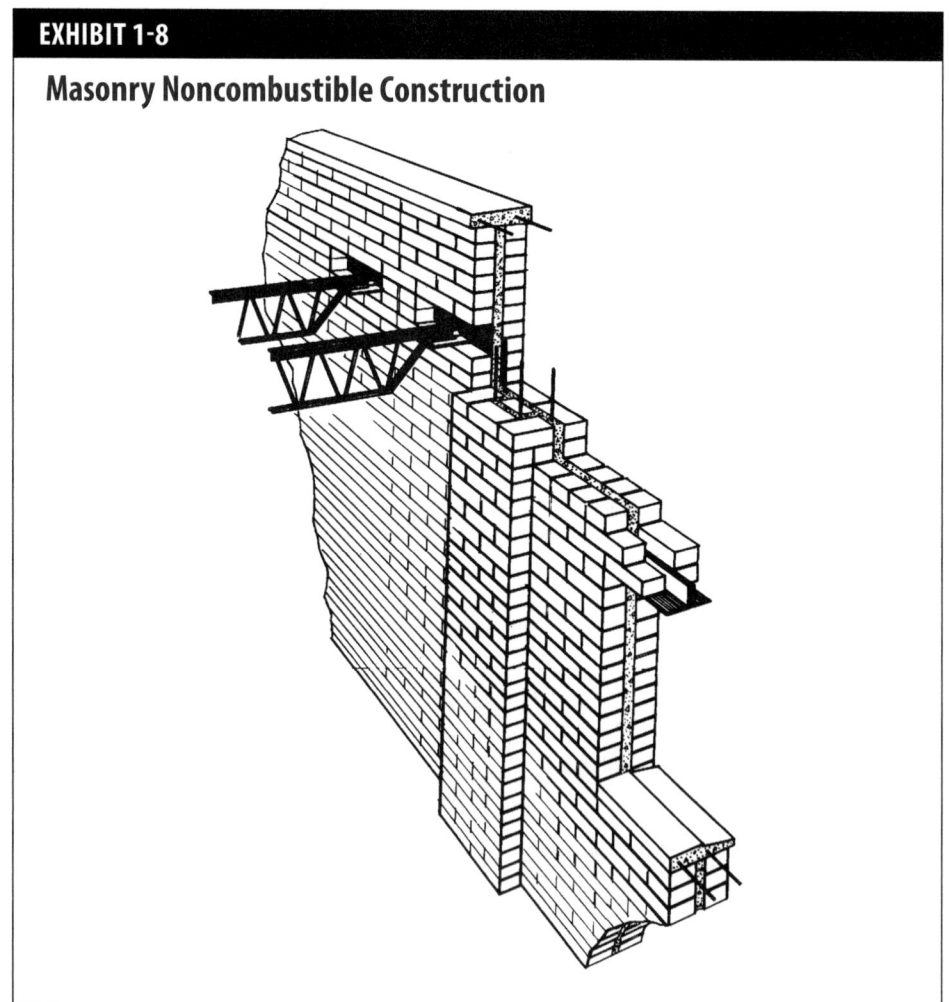

Reprinted with permission from *Stevens Valuation Quarterly* (Los Angeles: Marshall and Swift Publication Company, July 1973), pp. A-11 and A-12.

Fire-Resistive Construction

Fire-resistive construction (ISO Code 6) provides more fire protection than all other types of construction. Building materials used in fire-resistive construction resist heat longer than materials required for protected ordinary or noncombustible construction, but they do not resist it forever, and they do not keep fires from starting. Fire-resistive buildings can be severely damaged, even totally destroyed, by fire.

There is also construction known as **modified fire-resistive construction** (ISO Code 5). True fire-resistive construction requires certain thicknesses of masonry materials, and the fire-resistance rating of structural assemblies must be at least two hours. Modified fire-resistive construction may include masonry materials slightly deficient in thickness or structural assemblies with a fire-resistive rating of at least one hour but less than two hours.

Materials commonly used to meet fire-resistive requirements are reinforced concrete and protected structural steel for framing, reinforced concrete or masonry for bearing walls, and lighter noncombustible materials in other parts, such as curtain walls (walls that are enclosing but not load bearing).

> **Fire-resistive construction**
> A type of construction in which the building materials resist heat longer than materials required for noncombustible construction; the fire-resistance rating of structural assemblies in a fire-resistive building must be at least two hours.
>
> **Modified fire-resistive construction**
> A type of fire-resistive construction that is not as resistant to fire as is true fire-resistive construction; the fire-resistance rating of structural assemblies in a modified fire-resistive building is at least one hour but less than two hours.

Pre-Loss Fire Control Measures

Fires can be extinguished by removal of heat, fuel, or oxygen, or by breaking the chemical chain reaction. Apart from extinguishing efforts after fires start, many measures can be taken before a fire breaks out either to prevent fires from occurring or to minimize the severity of damage that fires can cause. Pre-loss fire control measures are based on these concepts:

- Controlling heat sources
- Separating heat sources from fuels
- Limiting vertical fire spread
- Limiting horizontal fire spread
- Full separation
- Substituting noncombustible materials for combustible ones
- Preventing arson

Controlling Heat Sources

In some cases, an organization's planned heat sources can be reduced or even eliminated. Thus, the risk control analyst should ask whether all the heat sources planned for energy are actually required. Where energy is needed, has care been taken to minimize the amount necessary? Are more furnaces, forges, kilns, or other heating devices in use than necessary? Are fires larger or hotter than necessary? Are flames used where another heat source (such as hot water) would do?

When heat is an unwanted by-product, various options are often available to control or dissipate it. For example, in lighting, fluorescent tubes are cooler than incandescent bulbs, and machines differ in the amount of friction heat they generate. The release of heat energy can be controlled by dissipating heat slowly through some kind of cooling substance or process.

The rate and path of electrical energy release can be controlled with proper fuses or automatic circuit breakers and with adequate grounding. Grounding can be used both to protect power circuits and to control static electricity created by moving machinery, liquids, and dust. It also applies to the mightiest unplanned electrical source—lightning—which can be controlled by lightning protection systems consisting of air terminals (lightning rods), down conductors, and grounding rods.

Separating Heat Sources From Fuels

Separating heat sources from fuels is a principal method of preventing hostile fires. The specific measures vary, depending on whether the heat sources are fixed or mobile.

When fixed-location heat sources have been identified, flammable or combustible materials must be kept away from them. NFPA and other organizations have developed standards that serve as a guide. Some involve only common sense. For example, the furnace room is not the place to keep trash, paper stocks, or janitors' materials. Other standards require more specific information. Building timbers and wood partitions should not be too close to furnaces and flues, but how close is too close? Here, recommendations are available from the NFPA and many insurers. Local and state building codes are usually very specific about separation distances for heating sources and fuels.

With stoves and other cooking appliances, the major fuel hazard (in addition to propane or natural gas) comes from cooking oils, greases, and fats in foods. Besides the immediate exposure, greasy deposits build up in hoods and flues—a frequent factor in restaurant fires. Regular removal of the buildup is a standard fire protection measure.

With electrical equipment, the first and most important separation device is enclosure and insulation of wiring, motor compartments, switches, and so on. Where arcing is possible—as in most electrical switches, motors, and generators—common sense dictates separation from flammable materials. When in the presence of a heat source, finely divided particles of any kind, including lint fibers, grain dust, saw dust, and certain metal dusts and shavings, can provide fuel for a fire. Lubricating greases and oils are other obvious fuels.

Buildings, equipment, and operations can be designed to keep fuels away from fixed heat sources. Because the exposure does not change rapidly, fire prevention plans are relatively easy to manage effectively. In contrast, the specific exposures for mobile heat sources (such as portable welding rigs or heaters) keep changing. The equipment has to be taken where it is needed and is not necessarily restricted to use in areas free of fuels. Furthermore, mobile equipment users can tend to underestimate the need to take elaborate precautions for an exposure that might last only a few minutes or even a few hours.

Limiting Vertical Fire Spread

Once a hostile fire starts inside a building, any barriers that serve, even temporarily, to separate the fire from additional fuel can help to reduce the fire's severity. A building's design can incorporate features intended to limit the vertical or horizontal spread of fire or even to achieve full separation of the building into two or more fire divisions.

Fire spread is enabled by vertical openings that allow heat to rise past combustible building components or contents. The most frequent examples of such vertical openings are stairwells and elevator shafts, ducts and flues, laundry and trash chutes, and openings used to allow pipes and wiring to get from floor to floor. Windows can also contribute to the spread of fire from one floor to another as the fire shoots out of one window and into the next one. This action is called "looping."

Another major exposure involves high stacking in storage. In many warehouses and stores, goods in cardboard containers are stacked up, row above row, for dozens of feet. Fires that start in lower rows are thus well supplied with fuel on which to grow.

Limiting vertical rise of fire is of prime importance in buildings designed for fire control. It is also important to maintain the integrity of fire barriers originally designed into a building. Although this principle should seem obvious, it is frequently violated. Conveyor belts may be installed to deliver goods from one floor to another, piercing what was a fire-resistive floor. Electrical, plumbing, or heating equipment may be installed leaving a large rough-cut opening through which fire can spread. Fire doors originally installed to separate passageways between stories may be damaged or blocked or may suffer from improper maintenance.

Openings through which building service lines (pipes, wires, ducts) pass should be filled with an appropriate type of noncombustible material. Masonry grout and commercially formulated fire stop caulking and gap filler are commonly used for this purpose. Of course, air ducts are designed to move air through a building, and when a hostile fire occurs, its hot gases can move through the building in the same way. Fire dampers, which can be activated by fire sensors, can be installed in ducts to stop the spread of fire and smoke.

Interior spaces in hollow walls and below floors (above ceilings) are other weak points. Finished walls in any type of construction may have open spaces. Open spaces between the floor of one story and the ceiling of the story below are standard features of frame and masonry construction and are common in

Fire stops
Solid pieces of material (usually wood) that are inserted between wall studs or other supporting members to delay the flow of heat through spaces that would otherwise be open.

finished areas of other building types. Because such spaces contribute significantly to the spread of fire, structural **fire stops** should be inserted. These are solid pieces running from support to support of a wall or floor. In frame buildings, fire stops inside walls often are wooden two-by-fours, running horizontally from stud to stud. Although such stops are combustible, they accomplish the purpose of delaying the flow of heat.

Attics are another hollow space in the path of rising heat. In row buildings, for example, fires starting in one unit can easily spread to adjoining units, despite masonry dividing walls, by spreading through the common attic. While fire-resistive materials such as brick and cement block are best for dividing walls, lighter materials can also delay spread until firefighters control the original fire.

Venting can reduce the spread of heat through an attic or along the underside of any roof or ceiling. Venting protects by cooling (controlling the rate of release of fire energy) and by directing the flow of heat into the open, away from combustibles in the building (a form of separation of heat from fuel). Built-in venting can prevent the sudden flaming that may occur when firefighters vent a building after a fire has already heated the interior.

Looping of fire from one story to the next through exterior windows is less common but can be serious. The generally recommended controls, commonly found in buildings of noncombustible and fire-resistive construction, are metal framing with wired glass or other installations that will not readily burn out, soften, or fall out in high heat. Another device is installation of fender walls that extend out between inline windows.

Limiting Horizontal Fire Spread

A fire may spread horizontally almost as easily as it spreads upward. Nearly all materials used to make walls, partitions, or doors in buildings have some value in slowing fire spread. (Unwired glass panels are a major exception.) Many plaster or wallboard partitions with wooden studs offer a nominal protection rating of one hour. In most fires, an hour's resistance means a contained fire. The problem, however, is that fires are not always noticed right away, making the difference between combustible and fire-resistive barriers an important consideration.

As with vertical separation, adequate horizontal separation calls for barriers with no holes for heat to get through. The ideal barrier is an unbroken wall that extends from the floor at the lowest level through and beyond the roof, with no windows near it in the exterior walls. Next in desirability is a wall with openings that are properly protected with fire doors. When the doors are not as fire resistant as the wall, then the strength of the whole wall is limited by the doors' strength. The doors should shut automatically when not in use, or they should be arranged to close themselves in the presence of fire heat, smoke, or the activation of the building's alarm system. Automatically closing equipment must not be blocked or rendered inoperable.

When equipment (such as a conveyor line) makes solid closure of walls impossible, special water-spray protection can be used. Special sprinklers are also needed where shafts cannot be fully enclosed (as with escalators, for example).

Full Separation

Full separation of a building into separate "fire divisions" can be achieved through the use of fire walls. Full separation is desirable between hazardous fire sources and less-hazardous operations, such as between manufacturing and office occupancies, and between operations involving materials with low autoignition temperatures or flash points and other materials. Full separation can also be achieved through the use of two (or more) buildings separated by clear space. Selected items of property (such as valuables) can be fully separated through the use of fire-resistive vaults.

A **fire wall** is a self-supporting solid wall that in most circumstances will prevent a fire from passing through or around it. To perform this function, a fire wall must have the appropriate fire-resistance rating and is therefore usually constructed of masonry materials, such as concrete or brick. A fire wall also must span the building's full width and height, from the lowest basement floor and through the roof to a specified height. A space in a building that is separated from other spaces in the building by a fire wall is referred to as a **fire division**.

Fire wall
A self-supporting solid wall that in most circumstances will prevent a fire from passing through or around it.

Fire division
A space in a building that is separated from other spaces in the building by a fire wall.

Another type of divider, called a "fire partition," is not as strong as a fire wall and usually does not extend from basement to roof. Although it can slow the spread of fire, a fire partition does not create fire divisions.

Fire walls sometimes have openings for utilities or for the movement of goods. Although these openings may be protected by sprinklers, they substantially reduce the reliability of the wall as a fire barrier because there is no assurance that the sprinklers will be functional when needed. Therefore, the possible spread of a fire from one side of the wall to the other (in other words, the absence of an actual fire division) must be taken into account.

Another way to achieve full separation is to have outdoor clear space separating two or more buildings. The amount of space necessary for reliable separation depends on the possible intensity of the exposing fire, the combustibility of the surfaces (walls and roofs), and the size and nature of windows and other openings in each building. The relative height of each of the two exposing buildings is also a factor.

Common standards for adequacy of clear spaces are based on the assumption that firefighters will arrive and be able to help protect the exposed building. If this assumption proves incorrect, the amount of clear space required is much greater. Additionally, the open space needs to be *clear*. Too frequently, the protective value of open spaces has been compromised or destroyed by clutter with combustible yard storage or by trees, grass, and brush growing between the structures. Wind, although not entirely predictable in speed or direction, should also be considered as a factor when addressing the potential for fire spread.

A fire-resistive vault provides full separation on a lesser scale. Valuable records, money, securities, jewelry, furs, or fine arts enclosed in a fire-resistive vault can often survive destruction of the rest of the building. To protect contents fully against fire, the vault must not only resist entry of flames but also insulate against temperature increases within the vault that could ignite or damage contents. It also must withstand rupture from collapse of the containing building. Lesser degrees of protection, as in a fire-resistive file cabinet with one-hour fire resistance, are still an improvement over ordinary cabinets.

Physical separation between records and their duplicates, which should be stored at totally different locations, is often the most practical method of controlling loss from fire damage to an organization's valuable papers and records.

Substituting Noncombustibles for Combustibles

Another method of fire control is substituting noncombustible materials for combustibles. With respect to the major components of buildings—as in the differences among wood frame, joisted masonry, noncombustible, and fire-resistive construction—organizations can choose noncombustibles when possible. Organizations can also consider substitution for special hazards, such as flammable and combustible liquids and gases. Combustibility is less frequently considered with ordinary property, such as desks and chairs. However, the use of steel instead of wood, or of heavy materials rather than light ones, can reduce both the likelihood and severity of damage. For example, hotels and hospitals can use noncombustible bedding, rugs, drapery, and furnishings.

Preventing Arson

Arson is the willful or malicious burning of property, usually with criminal or fraudulent intent. For risk control purposes, arson cases can be divided into crimes committed *against* the property owner and crimes committed *by* the property owner. Although insurers need to consider the possibility of both types, only arson against the owner is considered here.

The chance of an effective arson attempt is reduced when an arsonist's opportunity to enter the premises is made difficult and when an intruder's presence will be quickly detected. Locks, guards, alarms, and other systems effective in protecting against or detecting a burglar's forcible entry can also serve to prevent or detect an arsonist's entry. An organization should consider protective measures outside the premises as well. A structure's combustible exterior components, as well as its outside storage and refuse containers, can provide an opportunity for arson without the arsonist ever entering the building.

Sprinkler valves, fire alarm control devices, and similar protective devices can be secured so that any tampering by an arsonist will sound an alarm. Although alarms may not eliminate the arsonist's opportunity to set a fire, they can reduce the amount of time during which the arsonist can work undisturbed and they may enable firefighters to reach the scene even before a fire has been started.

Fire Extinguishment Methods

Fire protection engineers categorize the methods for extinguishing hostile fire into two principal groups: internal and external. Internal fire protection consists of measures an organization can take to extinguish fires on its own property. The most common forms of internal fire protection are automatic fire detection/suppression (sprinkler) systems, including their electronic and signaling components; portable fire extinguishers; standpipe systems; guard services; and fire brigades. External fire protection consists of fire departments and other public facilities that the community makes available to safeguard the general public from the spread of hostile fire.

Automatic Fire Detection/Suppression Systems

Automatic fire detection/suppression systems, commonly called "sprinkler systems," may use water, dry or wet chemicals, carbon dioxide, foam, or Halon™ (or its alternatives) as extinguishants. These automatic systems rely on fire detection devices to sense the presence of a hostile fire and on signaling devices to alert personnel on or off the premises to the danger. Many organizations supplement these systems with human resources in the form of guard services and fire brigades.

Every automatic sprinkler system consists of piping with discharging nozzles or heads, control valves and check valves for directing extinguishants within the system, gauges for monitoring pressure within the system, and alarm devices to signal when the system becomes operative. Some systems also have other monitoring alarms that call attention to any malfunction or disabling of the system so that it can be repaired. These automatic systems are classified by the types of extinguishants they use. The systems are described next, and their common uses are summarized in Exhibit 1-9. Water systems are the most common type. The other types are more costly and are used mainly to solve special problems.

> **EXHIBIT 1-9**
>
> ### Types of Automatic Suppression Systems and Common Uses
>
> **Water Systems**
>
> | | |
> |---|---|
> | Wet Pipe Sprinkler System | Wide range of occupancies with sufficient heat to prevent freezing of the system |
> | Dry Pipe Sprinkler System | Unheated buildings |
> | Deluge Sprinkler System | Quickly spreading fires, e.g., flammable liquids |
> | Preaction Sprinkler System | Occupancies unusually susceptible to water damage, e.g., computer rooms or libraries |
> | Water Spray Sprinkler System | Property that can be better protected by specially aimed nozzles, e.g., aircraft in hangars, combustible cooling towers, and chemical plant reactors |
> | Dry Chemical Systems | Occupancies exposed to Class B (flammable liquids) and Class C (electrical equipment) fires, e.g., dip tanks, flammable liquid storage areas, and spray booths |
> | Wet Chemical Systems | Commercial and residential cooking exposures, food processing plants, bulk petroleum terminals, non-bulk flammable liquid storage areas, and chemical process areas |
> | Carbon Dioxide Systems | Occupancies exposed to Class B or Class C fires that have appropriate mechanisms to evacuate humans and to close off the area to maintain the necessary concentration of CO^2 |
> | Halon and Halon Alternative Systems | Class A, B, and C fires in occupancies that are highly susceptible to water damage or chemical contamination, e.g., computer rooms, telephone equipment installations, and electrical control rooms |

Water Systems

Sprinkler systems that use water to extinguish fires are supplied from such sources as public water, gravity tanks, pressure tanks or—supported by an appropriate pump—in-ground tanks or natural bodies of water. The water is discharged from one or more sprinkler heads. Discharge occurs when a fire creates a sufficient level of heat to melt or break the sprinkler head operating mechanism (called a fusible link or frangible bulb), allowing the water to discharge. The water discharges upward (through an upright sprinkler head), downward (through a pendent sprinkler head), or sideways (through a sidewall sprinkler head), in each case striking a deflector that is designed to break up the waterstream into water droplets. This spray pattern covers a greater surface area to absorb the heat of the fire; cools the surrounding material and area; and confines, controls, and leads to extinguishment of the fire.

To conserve water in the system and to minimize water damage to property not endangered by fire, most systems allow only the sprinkler heads that are directly affected by the heat of the fire to open. The other sprinkler heads do not discharge unless their own fusible links or frangible bulbs melt or break.

The two basic types of water-based sprinkler systems are wet-pipe and dry-pipe systems. In a **wet-pipe system**, the piping is full of water and will immediately discharge water when the sprinkler head opens as a result of the melting or bursting of the fusible link or frangible bulb. Because the piping is filled with water at all times, the system responds faster than a dry-pipe system. However, also because of the water in the piping, a building with this type of system must be continuously heated to prevent the water from freezing.

In a **dry-pipe system**, the piping is filled with air under pressure. This air holds back a greater amount of water pressure through the use of an air clapper. The advantage of this type of system is that it can be installed in unheated buildings. The only area where heat is needed is around the dry-pipe valve, and this heat can be provided by enclosing the dry-pipe valve(s) in a noncombustible enclosure and heating the area(s) around the valve(s) with electric space heaters.

Dry-pipe systems have drawbacks. Because the piping is charged with air, once a sprinkler head is activated by fire, the air must be exhausted before any water can be discharged. In the resulting delay, more heads may be triggered than they would be with a wet-pipe system under similar conditions. Also, the dry-pipe system cannot protect as large a building area as a wet-pipe system can. For small, unheated areas within a building, a loop of piping filled with an anti-freeze solution can be used in lieu of a dry-pipe system.

In addition to wet-pipe and dry-pipe sprinkler systems, three other, more specialized types of water systems are available. With one of them, the **deluge system**, all the heads remain permanently open. Water is allowed into the system by a deluge valve, which in turn is activated by a separate detection system. Deluge systems protect against fires that could spread faster than conventional sprinkler heads can open, as in spills of flammable liquids.

A second alternative to basic sprinkler systems is a **preaction system**, which is the same as a deluge system except that the sprinkler heads normally are closed. Therefore, both the sprinkler heads and the detection components of a preaction system must operate before any water is released. Preaction systems are especially appropriate for occupancies that are unusually susceptible to water damage, such as computer rooms or libraries, or for areas with limited water supply.

A third alternative to basic sprinkler systems is a **water spray system**, which can have either open or closed nozzles. Instead of conventional sprinkler heads, these systems have directional nozzles specifically designed for the configuration of the space being protected and the hazards in that space. For example, water spray systems are used to safeguard aircraft in hangars, combustible cooling towers, and chemical plant reactors.

Wet-pipe system
A type of sprinkler system in which the piping is full of water and will immediately discharge water when a sprinkler head opens.

Dry-pipe system
A type of sprinkler system in which the piping is filled with air under pressure, holding back a greater amount of water pressure; when a sprinkler head opens, the air is released, allowing the water to flow through the piping to the head.

Deluge system
A type of sprinkler system in which all the heads remain permanently open; when activated by a detection system, a deluge valve allows water into the system.

Preaction system
A type of sprinkler system that is the same as a deluge system except that the sprinkler heads normally are closed; the sprinkler heads and the detection components must both operate before any water is released.

Water spray system
A type of sprinkler system that has directional nozzles specifically designed for the configuration of the space being protected and the hazards in that space.

Regardless of type, sprinkler systems must be properly designed to provide protection appropriate for the fire exposure. For example, a system installed in a low-hazard occupancy such as an office will not be adequate to provide the level of protection required for a tire warehouse. Moreover, the fact that a sprinkler system is present does not automatically guarantee that the system is adequate. It is essential to verify that the design and quality of the protection available is acceptable for the exposure.

Although water-based sprinkler systems usually function effectively, failures can occur for a number of recognized reasons, including these:

- Closed or inoperable control valves
- Inadequate maintenance and testing of the system
- Painted or obstructed sprinkler heads
- Inadequate water supply and pressure
- Hazards of occupancy exceeding the system's design capabilities

A sound fire risk control program should include specific steps to eliminate these and other problems that could lead water-based sprinkler systems to fail.

Dry Chemical Systems

Dry chemical system
A type of fire suppression system in which finely divided powders are distributed through pipes to nozzles positioned to allow for full distribution over the fire exposure area.

A **dry chemical system** contains finely divided powders stored in a cylinder. The cylinder is connected by pipes to nozzles positioned to fully distribute powder over the fire exposure area. The system can be activated by an automatic detection device, a fusible link, or manual release.

The dry chemical type of system is listed by Underwriters Laboratories for use on Class B (flammable liquid) and Class C (electrical equipment) fires. Thus, it has applications for exposures involving dip tanks, flammable liquid storage, and spray painting. When discharged, however, the dry chemicals leave a residue and are not suitable for areas housing computer operations or sensitive electronic testing equipment. Even if a dry chemical system protects an area near computer or electronic equipment, the discharge of the system and air movement in the building may cause some of the dry chemical to settle on the equipment and interfere with its functions. Dry chemical systems were commonly used for protecting cooking operations until 1994, when new standards called for the use of wet chemical extinguishing agents for Class K (cooking oil) fires.

Wet Chemical Systems

Wet chemical systems most commonly protect against fires in cooking equipment. Although wet chemical systems are similar in design to dry chemical systems, the extinguishing agent in a wet chemical system has several distinct advantages. When the wet chemical is discharged, a blanket of foam covers the burning fuel on the cooking surfaces and surrounding areas. The foam extinguishes the flames by forming a barrier between the liquid fuel and the oxygen. The foam also helps prevent further release of flammable vapors by lowering the fuel's temperature below its flash point. Because wet chemical agents are water-based and virtually nontoxic, they are also safer to use and significantly easier to clean up than dry powder. Portable wet chemical extinguishers (Class K) supplement a wet chemical system's suppression efforts.

Most wet chemical systems are found in commercial kitchens and bulk food processing operations, but they are also being installed in an increasing number of residential range hoods. Modern cooking appliances are designed to use vegetable oils, which require higher operating temperatures. Because dry chemical systems have been found to be less effective in extinguishing these higher temperature fires, the National Fire Protection Association now requires that fire protection systems for cooking appliances comply with the UL 300 standards of Underwriters Laboratories, Inc.

Wet chemical systems are also used for applications other than cooking. Firefighting foam is used in fixed (engineered) systems in which fuel products are dispensed or can be spilled, resulting in an incipient (beginning) stage fire, such as in bulk petroleum terminals, non-bulk flammable liquid storage rooms, and chemical process areas. Firefighting foam is also used by fire department personnel to fight flammable liquid fires that have progressed beyond the incipient stage. The wet chemical agent in smaller systems, such as those used to extinguish cooking fires, is stored in a pressure vessel ready to use. Applications requiring large amounts of wet chemical agent, or foam, typically store the wet chemical as a concentrate and mix it with water immediately before it is applied.

Carbon Dioxide Systems

In a **carbon dioxide system**, carbon dioxide is stored as a liquid under pressure and discharged as a gas through pipes to the fire site. The system is activated by an automatic detection device, a fusible link, or manual release.

Carbon dioxide system
A type of fire suppression system in which carbon dioxide is stored as a liquid under pressure and discharged as a gas through the pipes of the system to the fire site.

The carbon dioxide system is suited to the same types of Class B and Class C fires as is a dry chemical system. However, because the extinguishant changes into a gas when discharged and dissipates as it is released, enough of the agent must be present to extinguish the fire. For a total flooding system, such as for a flammable liquid storage room, all doors and vent openings to the area must be interconnected with the system so that when the system is activated, the openings are closed off to contain the carbon dioxide concentration within the protected area.

Carbon dioxide displaces the oxygen in the air and so smothers a fire. This displacement of oxygen can be dangerous when the system is protecting an area that may be occupied by employees. To protect personnel in such an area, a pre-alarm signal is necessary before the system activates to allow time for personnel to evacuate the area. Signs should be posted by the protected area's entrance and in the protected area advising of the type of protection and the necessity of leaving the area immediately if an alarm sounds.

Halon
A series of ionized hydrocarbon gases and liquids (halogenated hydrocarbons) that have the ability to halt chemical reactions and thus extinguish fires rapidly.

Halon (and Similar) Systems

The general term **halon** refers to a series of ionized hydrocarbon gases and liquids (halogenated hydrocarbons) that can extinguish fires rapidly by halting chemical reactions. Despite their excellent firefighting qualities, some halogenated hydrocarbons have been identified as stratospheric ozone-depletion agents. Accordingly, the United States Environmental Protection Agency prohibited production of Halon 1301 (the halon normally used in automatic fire extinguishment systems in the United States), as well as some other halons, after January 1, 1994.

The rules do not, however, prohibit the *use or sale* of Halon 1301. Current supplies of Halon 1301, as well as supplies of Halon 1301 recycled after production of Halon 1301 ceased, should make existing Halon 1301 systems usable for years to come. Although alternative agents for halon exist, none has been identified that can simply be charged into an existing halon system. The main problem is that greater quantities of the new agents are usually needed, and so larger storage tanks, larger pipe sizing, and different nozzles may be needed to achieve adequate discharge within the recommended time period. Accordingly, many organizations with existing Halon 1301 systems may choose to continue using those systems as long as they are able to obtain Halon 1301 at an affordable price.

However, halon alternative agents such as Inergen® are becoming increasingly popular in fire suppression systems. Inergen is a mixture of three inert gases—nitrogen, argon, and carbon dioxide—and extinguishes fire by lowering the oxygen content below the level that supports combustion but is sufficient to sustain human life. Therefore, these types of systems are safe for use in human-occupied facilities. The discussion that follows is equally descriptive of Halon 1301 systems and systems that use alternative agents.

The extinguishants used in these systems are effective on flammable liquids, electrical equipment, and surface fires in paper, wood, or other ordinary combustibles. These extinguishants put out fires very quickly, without water damage, and without contaminating the area. They are frequently used in computer rooms, telephone equipment installations, and other electrical control rooms.

One of the reasons for the widespread use of Halon 1301 is that it can extinguish fires with as little as a 5 percent concentration of halon in the air; it does not have harmful effects on humans below a 7 percent concentration, and it does not have long-lasting adverse effects on humans until they are exposed to a 10 percent concentration. However, a drawback of halon is its toxicity to humans and animals at certain concentrations. Other forms of halon are harmful at lower concentrations. In fact, the manufacturers of some of the alternatives to Halon 1301 have recommended the alternatives for use only in nonoccupied areas. A particular extinguishant's possibly harmful effects on humans or animals must always be considered before any system is installed.

Detection and Signaling Systems

Any extinguishant in an automatic suppression system is normally released only when that system is activated. Furthermore, these automatic systems usually need to be supplemented by human intervention from a public fire department or private fire brigade. Thus, two integral parts of every automatic suppression system are detectors to activate the system and signals to alert an outside fire department or internal brigade.

To be effective, detectors must be properly located; must respond to hostile fire, but not to extraneous, nonhazardous conditions; and must be designed for the structure in which they operate. In addition to activating suppression systems, alerting occupants, and summoning help, detectors have two particularly crucial purposes: to activate shutdown of air-handling systems in the event of smoke conditions and to release magnetic door closures to achieve separation.

Detectors may be designed to respond to heat, smoke, flame, gases, or to a combination of these. Choosing the appropriate type of detector during the design phase of a suppression system will ensure the correct response when danger truly exists but avoid false alarms. Fire safety engineers distinguish among these types of detectors:

- Fixed-temperature heat detectors—respond to a predetermined temperature level.
- Rate-of-rise detectors—respond to a predetermined rate of temperature rise.
- Smoke detectors—respond to smoke particles suspended in the air.
- Flame detectors—respond to the presence of flame in its very early stages.
- Gas-sensing fire detectors—respond to changes in the gas content of the environment during a fire.
- Combination detectors—contain more than one element that responds to a fire. For example, a heat detector may be designed to respond to either a fixed temperature or a particular rate of rise.

For the detection system to be effective, it must be properly maintained. It must also cover all building areas.

Adequate fire safety programs include action by people to put out the fire and to avoid further loss or damage. Therefore, one of the basic functions of virtually every automatic system is to emit a signal automatically to alert people to take appropriate actions. There are five basic categories of signaling systems, classified in terms of where the alarm signal is received:

- A **local system** rings only at the protected premises. The primary purpose is to notify occupants to evacuate the building. If the alarm rings outside during hours when the building is not occupied, action is required by a passing police officer or a "good Samaritan" to notify the fire department.

> **Local system**
> A type of signaling system that rings only at the protected premises.

Auxiliary system
A type of signaling system that is connected to an existing municipal fire alarm system on the same circuits that carry signals from the street fire alarm boxes.

Remote station system
A type of signaling system that transmits over a leased phone line from the protected property to a fire department or police department.

Proprietary system
A type of signaling system that alerts occupants on the protected property or on another facility of the same organization and that is staffed with the organization's own personnel trained to handle alarms.

Central station system
A signaling system that transmits to the premises of a company that is in the business of handling alarms.

- An **auxiliary system** is connected to an existing municipal fire alarm system on the same circuits that carry signals from the street fire alarm boxes. Any activation of this system causes the box alarm signal to be transmitted to the public fire department. The fire department ordinarily knows which alarm boxes are connected to auxiliary systems and can thus check for an alarm originating in the protected premises.
- A **remote station system** transmits over a leased phone line from the protected property to a fire department or police department. Before this type of system is chosen, the nature of the department's response should be determined. For example, it is vital that the police department's initial response to an alarm be to dispatch the fire department rather than to send police for investigative purposes.
- A **proprietary system** rings to alert occupants (or "proprietors") on protected property or at another facility of the same organization and staffed with its personnel trained to handle alarms. This system is a good arrangement for a large plant or one that has several buildings. Any alarm signal received permits the duty personnel to investigate and to take the necessary action, whether to restore the system after a needless alarm or to notify the fire department immediately.
- A **central station system** rings on the premises of a company that is in the business of handling alarms. The central station staff is trained in handling fire alarms and in notifying the proper fire department as well as notifying the individuals on the customer's call list.

Fire Extinguishers

Fire extinguishers are "first-aid" devices to control fire in its early stage. To be available for use, each extinguisher should be readily accessible, visible, properly inspected, and appropriate for the hazard. In many instances, the extinguisher may be used by an unskilled operator. Training is therefore an important element in the proper use of extinguishers and should include such topics as the extinguisher's location, its discharge range, its capabilities and limitations, and the method of putting it into operation. For hazardous operations, personnel should have training in the hands-on use of the extinguisher.

Fire extinguishers should be appropriate for the fires likely to occur. As shown in Exhibit 1-10, there are four classes of extinguishers.

Another crucial management responsibility is thorough, periodic inspection and maintenance of fire extinguishers. Maintenance requirements vary in their specifics and intervals with the type of extinguishant, and different extinguishers even in the same class require different inspection procedures. Good risk management requires determination of the inspection and maintenance requirements for each type of extinguisher, assurance that an employee of the organization or a qualified outside specialist performs this inspection and maintenance, and maintenance and checking of extinguisher inspection and maintenance records.

EXHIBIT 1-10

Types of Fire Extinguishers

Type	Extinguishant	For Fires Involving
Class A	Pressurized water and multipurpose dry chemical	Ordinary combustible materials, such as paper and wood
Class B	Ordinary dry chemical, multipurpose dry chemical, foam, carbon dioxide, and Halon 1211	Flammable liquids and gases, such as gasoline, acetone, and propane
Class C	The same as for Class B with the important criterion that the extinguishant be a nonconductor of electricity	Energized electrical equipment
Class D	Dry powder agent specifically listed for use on the particular combustible metal that is on fire	Combustible metals, such as magnesium, sodium, and lithium

Standpipe Systems

A **standpipe system** is a series of pipes that run throughout a building and supply water to hoses that can be attached to valves in the standpipes. Standpipe systems, which can be used by an organization's specially trained firefighting personnel or a public fire department, increase the efficiency with which a human-operated fire extinguishing system can distribute water. Standpipe protection plays an especially important role in getting firefighting hose lines deployed to upper floors or other interior areas that are too distant to be reached from the street level. Thus, installation and maintenance of a standpipe system is essential for fire protection in high-rise structures.

Standpipe system
A series of pipes running throughout a building through which water can be supplied to fire hoses.

Guard Services

Guard services are another means of providing internal fire protection. Guard services may be provided either through a contract service or by employees of the facility. One or more guards tour the property and preferably use a portable clock to verify that they have visited each station. Guards should follow designated routes so that each area of the facility is checked on a definite frequency, building areas are secured, fire hazards are identified and reported, continuous production processes are monitored, fire protection equipment is checked, and the proper authorities are notified if fire is discovered. Follow-up procedures by management or supervisory personnel should verify that the clock stations are being visited at prescribed times and that the guards are performing their functions.

Fire Brigades

Every facility should have a fire emergency plan that includes some form of fire brigade activity. The brigade can range from a few individuals responsible for notifying the fire department, initiating evacuation, securing areas, and removing important files that may be in the danger area, to a complete fire crew, with a fire chief and assistants, capable of initiating and maintaining an effective attack on a fire.

To determine the appropriate size of a fire brigade for a specific facility, one should evaluate the fire potential, the existing on-site protection, the potential magnitude of a fire, and the available public fire protection. With this information, the organization's risk management staff can design a plan in cooperation with plant personnel and management to include the number of people on the team, designated crew leaders, and guidelines for the crew's functions and duties. The plan should also outline the training required to make the brigade an effective part of the overall fire protection program.

External Fire Protection

External fire protection—the public fire department—is capable of protecting a facility only when a reliable water supply is reasonably accessible and has adequate water volume and pressure, and when fire department personnel are capable of responding to a fire at the facility. Generally, the most reliable water supply is a fire hydrant connected to a municipal water system. Other sources of water, although less reliable and of limited quantity, include dry hydrants at lakes or rivers, fire department tanker shuttles, and private water storage tanks.

Fire hydrants must be available to the premises and must be within 500 to 1,000 feet road distance to the premises (not "as the crow flies"). Besides the hydrant locations, the underground water mains and available water supply must be considered. Accordingly, an organization must test water supplies to verify the available supply and pressure before beginning new construction or making changes in existing operations. Such changes could increase the fire hazard potential, which might, in turn, require higher water supply and pressure requirements. Proper fact-finding procedures will reveal whether the water supply is adequate. If inadequacies are discovered, supplemental supplies must be developed for adequate protection. Identifying problems before finalizing construction plans is better than discovering deficiencies after plans have been completed or construction is under way.

A problem that sometimes arises with large and special exposures is failure to acquaint public fire department personnel with plant layout, hazards, and firefighting resources before a fire occurs. When a fire occurs, this lack of pre-loss planning can delay firefighting efforts or even lead to ineffective or dangerous courses of action. For example, firefighters might apply water to a substance that reacts violently with water, or they might become lost or trapped in an unfamiliar building.

Personnel responsible for fire safety can develop readiness programs in cooperation with their local fire department. Any such program should inform the fire department of specific items like building floor plans, locations of exits, what hazardous materials are present, and where such materials are located. In many cases, the fire department will visit the site to inspect the premises and will determine where water supplies are located.

Controlling Water Damage

Most manual firefighting is done with water, and occasionally the water causes more property damage than the fire. (Of course, if no water were applied, the fire would do more damage—a point sometimes overlooked.) Also, automatic sprinklers sometimes release water when there is no fire, with some resulting damage.

Control starts with sources. Sprinkler systems should be properly designed, installed, and maintained. Some automatic sprinkler systems are designed to be less likely to respond to stimuli from sources other than hostile fires. For example, different sprinkler heads will open at different temperatures. Sprinkler heads that do not respond to ambient temperatures produced by normal operations should be chosen, and vulnerable sprinkler heads should have guards installed that reduce the probability of accidental damage.

Also important in reducing water damage loss severity is to provide means for water to move out of a building with minimum damage. Impermeable floors, with drains to channel the water outside, are common means of control. Skids or pallets that keep stock off the floor also help to reduce water damage losses.

Most sprinkler systems have waterflow alarms that sound when water begins to flow through the system. Their primary purpose is to serve as a fire alarm. However, such alarms also provide prompt notification of an accidental discharge from a sprinkler system. Additionally, sprinklers can be designed to withhold or interrupt water flow unless combinations of stimuli are received that confirm the presence of a hostile fire. For example, one type of sprinkler head automatically shuts off when the temperature cools, thus enabling it to extinguish a small fire and then cease spraying. Because they are expensive, such heads are not frequently installed but are used in special applications.

A common practice to prevent water damage is to minimize the amount of water-damageable property kept in basements or in rooms below those with serious fire exposure or another source of potential water damage.

Finally, where the possible loss from water damage is large, automatic extinguishing systems using extinguishants other than water may be used. Preaction systems, although they contain water, can also reduce, but not eliminate, the possibility of water damage.

Experience has shown that the danger of water damage from sprinklers has often been overestimated. Computer equipment, for example, is often assumed to be highly damageable by water from sprinklers. However, prompt drying and cleaning of computer equipment by restoration specialists can greatly minimize any water damage loss.

After the Fire Is Out

Loss control continues to be possible after a fire is out. Property losses can be minimized by good salvage techniques, and business interruption losses can be minimized by using alternate resources or by expediting repairs.

Fire salvage is a specialized skill. For anyone who rarely deals with fire losses, an experienced salvage contractor's services are needed. The contractor may be supplied by an insurer or can be hired directly.

Alternate resources may be arranged in advance by having standby equipment and facilities at another location. For some organizations, competitors' facilities may be available; occasionally organizations even have pre-loss understandings of mutual aid. More often, an organization will have to find vacant facilities and adapt them to its needs. Of course, temporary operation requires financing in addition to outlay of money for repair and reconstruction. Whether operations can be continued may depend on whether arrangements for risk financing have been adequate to cover all these expenditures.

Organized efforts to ensure that appropriate loss reduction measures will be taken at the time of, and immediately following, a severe fire or another catastrophe are known as crisis management or disaster planning. Effective crisis management requires extensive planning and practice *before* any crisis occurs.

Life Safety in Fires

Life safety engineers have developed extensive sets of fire safety standards for particular kinds of buildings. These standards have been codified in the *Life Safety Code*® published by the National Fire Protection Association and incorporated explicitly or by reference into the statutes and ordinances of most localities in the United States. Therefore, compliance with the applicable sections of the *Life Safety Code* usually is a legal requirement; failure to comply is not only a breach of an ordinance (bringing fines and other penalties) but also can be substantial evidence of negligence in failing to adequately safeguard others from injury or damage by fire. Consequently, not complying with the *Code* increases the likelihood not only of property and personnel losses but also of liability losses.

Therefore, an important risk management function of every organization is to determine, and comply with, the provisions of the *Life Safety Code* (and local ordinances) that govern the life safety features of the building(s) the organization owns or occupies.

Life Safety Code® is a registered trademark of the National Fire Protection Association, Inc., Quincy, Mass. 02269.

RISK CONTROL FOR THEFT LOSSES

In its various forms, theft is one of the most severe and pervasive causes of property loss. The term "theft" is generally understood to include any act of stealing. Different types of theft are described by various labels, such as burglary, robbery, employee theft or dishonesty, extortion, fraud, forgery, alteration, looting, shoplifting, pilferage, and trickery.

Any type of property may be targeted for theft. However, thieves are most attracted to money or any other property that has high value and low weight and can be easily converted to cash. Cigarettes, liquor, drugs, food, and electronics are examples of target commodities. The main loss consequence of theft is loss of value of the stolen property. However, when computer equipment is stolen, valuable information (such as trade secrets or customer lists) stored in the equipment is also lost. Other consequences include property damage resulting from breaking and entering, vandalism during the commission of a theft, loss of business income, and extra expenses.

Theft risk control often focuses on burglary, robbery, and employee theft losses, three of the most common types of theft:

- Burglary is generally defined as theft by someone who forcibly enters the place where the property is kept.
- Robbery, or "hold-up," involves the use (or threat) of force against the person from whom the property is taken.
- Employee theft (also called employee dishonesty or embezzlement) is theft that an employee commits against his or her own employer.

Although these terms are defined more specifically in crime insurance policies, the general definitions given here are adequate for the purpose of examining risk control measures against common types of theft.

In most cases, the probable severity of a theft loss is less than that from other property exposures. A fire may destroy an entire building and its contents, but a thief is likely to steal only a small percentage of the total contents. Likewise, theft of cash in any one occurrence is limited to the amount of cash on hand—an observation that suggests either eliminating or limiting the cash. Despite the possibly lower severity of crime losses, the overall frequency of theft losses may be greater than the frequency of fire losses, suggesting that loss prevention can be effective.

Unlike many other theft losses, employee theft losses can be very severe. In some cases, trusted employees (particularly officers) have taken so much that the organization's survival was threatened.

Risk Control for Burglary and Robbery Losses

Protective measures against burglary and robbery losses may be divided roughly into four groups. All of these measures can play an important role as deterrents to would-be intruders:

- Physical protection to premises in order to delay access by criminals
- Installation of alarm systems and other devices or the use of guards or security patrols to indicate when outsiders have gained access to the premises
- Use of automatic cameras or closed-circuit television systems to help identify criminals in order to facilitate their arrest and conviction
- Various protective procedures, including procedures for handling money and securities, that will reduce the likelihood of theft or the amount of property accessible to thieves

Physical Protection

Physical protection measures include passive restraints to entry of a building and the use of safes and vaults for protecting valuables.

A businessowner can install passive restraints to entry. For example, the type of lock used on doorways can make a difference of several minutes in the entry time needed by a thief. Some ordinary locks can be manipulated in a matter of seconds. A deadbolt lock cannot be manipulated as quickly and usually requires the picking of the tumblers or the use of force.

The rear doors in a store or an office can be barred from the inside so that access is difficult. Bars, gates, and grills can be put across windows or doorways. In selecting such measures, however, the risk analyst should remember that any measure that impedes burglars' entry or exit may also serve to impede firefighters' entry or the public's emergency exit.

A common type of theft called "smash and grab" involves breaking a show window and grabbing valuable items. Ordinary plate glass is easily broken. Varieties of breakage-resistant glass and plastic materials often improve protection, particularly for smaller windows. In jewelry display windows, another device effectively impedes a burglar's access to a show window display: a sheet of breakage-resistant glass suspended behind the show window glass. This second sheet is hung on chains from the top of the show window so that it swings backward when struck. The show window can be broken, but the second sheet of glass is difficult to break, because of its composition and because it swings. It is difficult for a thief to reach around the second sheet of glass when it is properly installed.

The installation of good locks, gates, bars, breakage-resistant glass, and similar devices may provide satisfactory protection in most cases for mercantile stocks of low value especially if the premises are under frequent surveillance by police and in a low-crime area. However, such passive restraints may merely delay a burglar's entrance and do not guarantee that no burglaries will occur. The adequacy of such measures also must be considered in light of the values involved. Small volume, low weight, and high value make merchandise particularly attractive to a burglar. Safes or vaults may be more effective for protecting such property against burglars.

Safes vary in their vulnerability to burglary. Many safes are basically fire protection devices, referred to as record safes. Record safes are designed to protect money and valuable records from fire damage; they offer little resistance to burglars. Money safes are designed to be burglar resistive. Within each category, different types of safes offer different degrees of resistance to fire and burglary. Safes can be most readily classified by reference to the Underwriters Laboratories label found inside the door of most quality safes.

Vaults are rooms or compartments designed to protect valuable property against theft, fire, and perhaps other causes of loss. Typically, a vault's walls are constructed of steel, or concrete lined with steel, and the door to the vault is constructed of steel with a lock. Like safes, vaults provide varying degrees of protection depending on how thick their walls and doors are and the quality of their locks. Vaults, because they can be larger than safes, can be used to protect items such as furs, valuable rugs, fine arts, and other bulky items.

Safes and vaults, like other physical protective devices, do not eliminate the possibility of a loss. They must be used properly to achieve the desired results. At appropriate times, valuable items must be put in safes or vaults, and the combinations (or keys) must not be spread around or readily accessible.

Alarm Systems

Unlike some physical protection devices, alarm systems do not prevent burglars from entering. Except to the extent that they serve as a deterrent, the purpose of such systems is to indicate when an intruder has entered the premises.

A simple alarm system consists of electrical contact switches or metallic foil on each door, window, or other opening into the building. Usually, the system is wired so that an electrical current passes through the system constantly. Opening a door or window interrupts the electrical current, which activates an alarm system. This is a **perimeter system**: its intent is to trigger an alarm whenever unauthorized entry is made into the building. In addition to contact switches and metallic foils, other detection devices used in perimeter systems include photoelectric detectors, vibration detectors, and glass breakage detectors.

In addition to perimeter protection, some burglar alarm systems protect specific areas within a facility and are therefore referred to as **area protection** or **space protection**. Detection devices used for area protection include photoelectric detectors; sound detectors; and motion detection devices, such as ultrasonic, microwave, or passive infrared motion detectors.

Perimeter system
A type of burglar alarm system that is designed to signal an alarm whenever unauthorized entry is made into the building.

Area protection (space protection)
Protection that a burglar alarm system can provide by detecting entry into specific areas within a facility.

Object protection
Protection that a burglar alarm system can provide by detecting a burglar's efforts to enter or steal specific objects such as safes, vaults, display cases, or works of art.

Burglar alarm systems can also be configured to protect specific objects that burglars are likely to target, such as safes, vaults, filing cabinets, display cases, and works of art. This type of protection, referred to as **object protection**, is usually provided in combination with perimeter or area protection. Detection devices commonly used for object protection include contact switches, vibration detectors, sound detectors, and smoke and heat detectors. (Smoke and heat are generated when a burglar tries to break into a safe or vault using a torch.)

In addition to detection devices, a burglar alarm system consists of a control unit and a reporting device. On receiving an alarm signal from a detection device, the control unit communicates with the reporting device to set off an alarm. Essentially the same options for setting off a fire alarm are available for setting off a burglar alarm. Of the two most commonly used types of alarms—local and central station—central station alarms are more effective.

Holdup alarm
A type of burglar alarm situated so that it can be triggered by a bank teller or store clerk during a robbery, sending an alarm signal to a central station company or the police.

Alarms are not limited to burglary prevention. Alarm systems may also be used to reduce the robbery exposure. **Holdup alarms** (triggered by buttons or foot pedals) can be situated so that a bank teller or store clerk can trigger them, sending an alarm signal to a central station company or to the police. (The alarm is silent at the location being robbed.) If rapid response is possible, the police may arrive while a robber is still on the premises. The value of holdup alarms should be weighed against the possibly increased danger of a robber's harming employees at the site if the police arrive while the robber is still there or if the robber detects that an employee has set off an alarm.

Alarm systems vary as to their quality and extent of protection. Insurers generally give credits only for approved alarm systems. An approved system is one installed by a burglar alarm company approved by the insurer. Underwriters Laboratories, Inc., issues alarm certificates that indicate the grade, type, and extent of the alarm system, and these certificates are considered in granting insurance rate credits. No matter how expensive it is, an alarm system without an Underwriters Laboratories certificate may receive no premium reduction, a fact too often discovered only after money has been spent on an alarm system.

One of the most difficult problems with burglar alarms is false alarms caused by accidental triggering. Because of the high frequency of false alarms, police in some cities assign a low priority to calls that come in from burglar alarm systems, and they may issue citations and impose fines if they are called to respond to an excessive number of false alarms. In many municipalities, this number may be as low as two or three false alarms in a given year. A central station alarm company's services can greatly reduce this problem because the alarm company can help verify whether an actual break-in has occurred.

Another deficiency is that an alarm system does not stop burglaries from occurring—it merely shortens the burglar's operating time. A delay of five to fifteen minutes or more can occur from the time an alarm is given until a guard or police officer can reach the premises. This may be enough time for the burglars to complete their work.

Guards or Security Patrols

Many organizations find it worthwhile to maintain guard service on their premises. A guard goes through the building at periodic intervals (such as hourly) to see that everything is in good order. Although the presence of the guard can be a deterrent to burglars, it by no means eliminates the possibility of loss.

Central station alarm companies also maintain a **supervised system** under which the guard signals to the central station upon visiting each station throughout the premises. These systems are arranged so that the alarm company sends an emergency runner to the premises if the guard fails to signal as required. Sometimes burglars or robbers will force a guard to continue making rounds while a theft is underway. Most signaling systems include an arrangement whereby the guard can secretly signal for help even while making rounds under the burglar's scrutiny.

> **Supervised system**
> A type of burglar alarm system in which a guard at the protected premises signals to a central station upon visiting each station throughout the premises; if the guard fails to signal as required, an emergency runner is sent to the premises.

Surveillance Cameras

Banks, twenty-four-hour convenience stores, and other firms with high robbery exposure frequently install automatic cameras to photograph criminals in the process of committing a crime. Such installations are effective in two ways:

- They facilitate the identification and conviction of criminals after the offense has been committed, making the offenders unavailable for future offenses, at least for a short time.
- The increased probability of identification and conviction discourages robbery.

Protective Procedures

A property owner can institute many procedures in addition to using the devices just described. One simple procedure many merchants use is to locate the safe or other valuable property where it can be observed by police patrols from outside the building. Sufficient lighting is left on to illuminate the property during night hours.

Another common procedure is for some businesses to accept only credit cards, or cash that does not exceed the purchase price by more than a small amount, thus avoiding having large amounts of money in the cash register. Incoming money is immediately deposited through a one-way slot or chute into a burglar-resistant safe. Robbers tend to target isolated businesses with large amounts of money or other attractive property and limited personnel. Steps that reduce isolation, reduce the amount of money or other attractive property on hand, and increase the number of employees on duty tend to reduce the likelihood of a robbery.

Organizations that handle large quantities of money or securities may arrange for frequent deposits at a bank. This results in a smaller value on the premises at any one time and smaller quantities carried by messengers to the bank. Many organizations also transport money, securities, and other valuable property by an armored car messenger service.

Risk Control for Employee Theft Losses

Although many employees commit petty thefts of office supplies, long-distance personal telephone calls, and the like, the targets of serious employee theft are money, high-valued merchandise, and intellectual property assets such as trade secrets and other proprietary information. Losses caused by an organization's own employees are also referred to as embezzlement and employee dishonesty. One source has estimated U.S. employers' losses because of occupational fraud (defined similarly to employee theft) at over $600 billion a year, an amount that far exceeds total U.S. fire losses annually.[1]

Many risk control measures that reduce outsiders' opportunities for taking property do not prevent most of the losses committed by employees. Employees are already present on the premises, and the employer's property is necessarily committed to their care. Also, employees understand the employer's procedures and vulnerabilities. And some employees are vested with a great deal of responsibility and authority in the organization, with accompanying knowledge of its procedures and vulnerabilities. Thus, different strategies and methods of risk control are needed.

Research has shown that the single most important factor affecting whether employees will take good care of their employer's interests, including property, is how they feel about their supervisors. Examples set by managers are also important. When bosses pad their expense accounts, take products home, or otherwise act against the organization, people under them are likely to do the same. Although good rapport and good examples are the first lines of defense, they are not foolproof. For this and other good management reasons, organizations should have well-designed accounting and access controls. Exhibit 1-11 presents one method of categorizing internal theft prevention systems. The top half of the chart depicts measures that increase the probability of quick discovery. Because these measures are based on the assumption that some thefts may happen despite good rapport between employees and management, they are labeled "low-trust measures." Low-trust measures include accounting controls and access controls.

Accounting control
A low-trust measure intended to limit employee theft losses by keeping track of cash flows and detecting any improprieties.

Access control
A low-trust measure intended to reduce employee theft losses by limiting access to target property to a limited number of key employees.

- **Accounting controls**, which keep track of cash flows and detect any improprieties, limit loss caused by manipulating a firm's records. Examples of such controls include internal auditing, patrolling, observing, leaving audit trails, and enforcing the use of standardized procedures.
- **Access controls** reduce losses of merchandise and other property (including currency and coins, confidential documents, and trade secrets) by limiting access to target property to a limited number of key employees. Locked entrances, armed guards, and both photo and electronic identification badges may be among the devices used to limit access to extremely valuable property and information. Keys, safe combinations, and electronic access codes and passwords are usually given to only a limited number of employees. Authority to sign checks, purchase orders, and contracts is given only to selected employees who cannot operate without this access.

Property Risk Control 1.39

EXHIBIT 1-11
An Internal Theft Prevention System

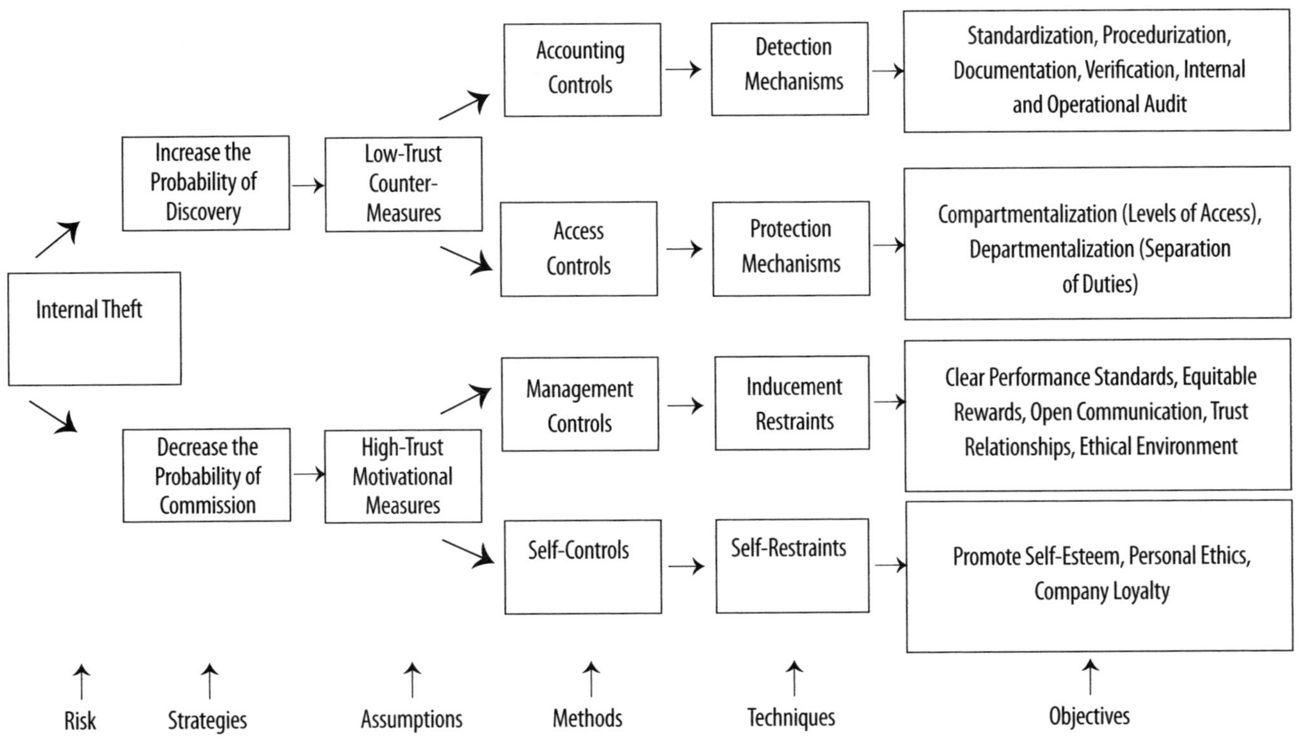

Risk	Strategies	Assumptions	Methods	Techniques	Objectives
Internal Theft	Increase the Probability of Discovery	Low-Trust Counter-Measures	Accounting Controls	Detection Mechanisms	Standardization, Procedurization, Documentation, Verification, Internal and Operational Audit
			Access Controls	Protection Mechanisms	Compartmentalization (Levels of Access), Departmentalization (Separation of Duties)
	Decrease the Probability of Commission	High-Trust Motivational Measures	Management Controls	Inducement Restraints	Clear Performance Standards, Equitable Rewards, Open Communication, Trust Relationships, Ethical Environment
			Self-Controls	Self-Restraints	Promote Self-Esteem, Personal Ethics, Company Loyalty

Adapted with permission from Jack Bologna, "A New Look at the Internal Theft Prevention Process," *Assets Protection*, Sept./Oct. 1980, p. 33.

Background Checks

Employers can prevent employee theft losses by not employing dishonest people. A key ingredient in screening out dishonest people is gathering information about job applicants and checking references before hiring. To be effective, information regarding a prospective employee's background should be supplied by sources other than the applicant.

Separation of Duties

Separation of duties is another important strategy in many programs to control employee theft. The majority of employee thefts involve one employee acting alone. Proper separation of duties makes it difficult for any one employee to steal (or to steal a great deal) without the collaboration or cooperation of at least one other employee. Some basic approaches to using separation of duties include these guidelines:

- No single employee should have complete control of every aspect of a transaction or a sensitive task. For example, employees who maintain inventory records should not be the same employees who physically count inventory.
- Work should flow from one employee to another so that the second employee's work acts as a check on the first employee's work. For example, in a warehouse, Employee A takes property for shipment to the loading dock, and Employee B loads it onto a truck. Both employees keep tallies, and their tallies must agree.
- Employees who perform record keeping and bookkeeping duties should not also be responsible for the handling and custody of the organization's assets. For example, an accounts receivable clerk should not also be entrusted with opening mail that might contain payments to the organization.

RISK CONTROL FOR OTHER CAUSES OF LOSS

Risk control measures for other important causes of loss—explosion, windstorm, flood, and earthquake—can provide additional protection for organizations.

Explosion

Many explosions have the chemistry of extremely rapid combustion—in essence, nearly instantaneous fire over the whole of a large quantity of material. Examples include explosions of flammable liquid vapors and gases, dust explosions (such as grain elevator explosions), and the action of commercial explosives. The principles of explosion control are similar to those for the slower combustion of fires. A major difference is the much shorter time available for explosion counteraction.

Explosion suppressors can act effectively the instant an explosion is initiated. Such suppression equipment detects a sudden abnormal increase in pressure and automatically floods the incipient explosion with a suppressing agent. This equipment resembles an automatic fire extinguishing system but differs in the type of detection and the extreme rapidity of response.

Explosive materials should be properly handled to prevent initial combustion that could lead to explosion. Sometimes, in addition, the material may be kept in a low-oxygen or an oxygen-free atmosphere, in which much or all of the air in a chamber is replaced with inert gas, such as carbon dioxide or nitrogen. Self-oxidizing compounds can, however, still burn or explode in the absence of atmospheric oxygen. Similar treatment may be provided for electrical equipment, or electrical equipment may be of explosion-proof design appropriate for an explosive environment.

For explosions that are not prevented or suppressed, venting is the standard method of control—using solid barriers, such as an earthen bank, to direct the force toward open air and away from other property. Thus, for example, dynamite is often stored in structures, called "igloos," with concrete or steel walls and light roofs (so the explosive force is directed upwards). For further protection, the igloos may be surrounded by earth or concrete banks.

Explosion of pressure vessels, such as steam boilers, is another major type of explosion. Explosions occur in such equipment when the pressure exerted exceeds the vessel's capacity to contain pressure because of either an increase in the amount of pressure or a decrease in the vessel's strength. Changes in strength or pressure must therefore be prevented or controlled. Proper operation, maintenance, and inspection are the keys to preventing explosions or other breakdowns of such equipment.

Windstorm

Although the energy source in windstorms cannot be controlled, a business can choose to locate away from areas with frequent severe storms, such as hurricanes and tornadoes. However, it is often impractical to select locations purely on the basis of windstorm exposure, and no location above ground avoids windstorms completely.

Some buildings resist damage from wind better than others. Most well-engineered and maintained structures generally will not incur damage from winds below fifty miles per hour. Higher gusts and higher sustained wind velocity are relatively common. Plate glass, attached exterior trim, and roofing are particularly susceptible to windstorm damage. Ordinarily, glass is damaged by windblown objects. However, a high-velocity wind alone can break glass, tear away exterior trim, and create forces that tend to lift the roof. If the roof is not adequately anchored, it can blow off, and exposed contents can be damaged or destroyed. Even when the roof holds, its surface can suffer considerable stress, with damage to shingles, tiles, or other attached coverings.

Pre-loss actions for windstorm include these:

- Design buildings and outside structures to withstand anticipated wind loads. The design should reflect location conditions in which wind velocities might exceed the average.
- Provide storm shutters and blinds for windows and other openings rated to handle higher wind loads.
- Maintain roof and wall systems, including roof tie-downs, in good repair and provide adequate supports for outside structures.
- Secure materials and equipment located outside the facility.
- Locate trees and utility poles away from buildings.

Post-loss actions for windstorm include these:

- Use spare materials such as plywood panels, tarpaulins, and plastic sheets to temporarily repair damage to buildings and avoid exposing the building's interior and its contents to the elements.
- Patrol the premises to prevent looting or vandalism.

Flood

Water damage may be caused when low elevation is combined with rising water levels. In major hurricanes, flooding often causes more damage than does the force of wind. Natural flooding, whether from hurricanes or other storms, or from other weather-related events may be classified as three types:

- Flooding from high tides
- Flooding from rising water in rivers, streams, and lakes
- Flooding from inadequate runoff of rain water (flash floods)

The best method of treating this exposure is to avoid locating in areas known to have had flood experience. Because construction and rearrangement of the landscape changes natural runoff and flood patterns, consideration has to be given to how these new patterns may affect property. The consideration should, of course, occur before construction begins.

Where property is exposed to high water, grounds and buildings should be designed to take this exposure into account, as should location of property in the building.

Many risk control measures are possible, including these:

- Dams and other impoundments of water can be placed to cause, modify, or reduce energy buildup.
- The rate and direction of release of water energy can be controlled by creating channels and impoundments to direct the runoff and by creating open areas over which flooded waters can spread out, reducing their depth and speed of flow.

- Dikes and other barriers can separate flood waters from property (and people) to be protected. Channels can also achieve such separation. Elevating property (on high ground or in upper stories of a building) is another example of separating property from flood waters.
- Property may be designed to resist the pressure of flood waters and the effects of dampness. Structures can be made more solid, with shapes that enhance water flow around and past them. Providing means to allow for runoff or pumping out water when the flood has subsided may also be necessary. (Dikes and levees sometimes increase loss by keeping water impounded longer.)
- Buildings in flood-prone areas can be constructed so that the lowest floor is above the 100-year flood level. (The 100-year flood level is a statistic that indicated, for a particular place, the magnitude of flooding that can be expected to occur on average with a frequency of once every 100 years.) On beachfront properties, construction on pilings serves not only to elevate the structure but also to withstand the pressure of waves.
- Counteraction includes such activities as emergency sandbagging, moving property to higher levels, speeding draining by pumping, and promptly drying and cleaning damaged property to minimize adverse effects.

Earthquake

As a practical matter, little attention is paid to earthquake loss control except in geographic areas that have had a history of damaging earthquakes. Where a serious earthquake exposure exists, an earthquake's effects can be reduced by careful attention to building design and construction, taking into consideration the conditions of the soil upon which the building will rest.

Earthquake-resistant buildings are designed so that the structure as a whole will withstand the forces of earth movement. Most building collapses occur from the violent side-to-side, or lateral, shaking associated with earthquakes. The most common design for an earthquake-resistant building is a rigid structure with walls, columns, and pillars tied securely to floors and roofs by horizontal, vertical, and cross members carried through to the foundations. Construction of some modern high-rise buildings allows them to sway with an earthquake, thereby absorbing the force exerted on the building.

SUMMARY

Risk management is concerned with the treatment of loss exposures to prevent accidental losses from interfering with an organization's objectives. Appropriate risk control measures can prevent or reduce the severity of many accidental losses, such as property losses caused by fire, theft, explosion, windstorm, flooding, and earthquake.

A fire must have an initial source of heat, oxygen, and fuel, as well as an uninterrupted chain reaction. Fire prevention efforts focus on removing one or more of these elements from the scene. Heat sources may result from electrical, chemical, mechanical, or nuclear heat energy. The source of oxygen for most fires is ordinary air—the better the supply of oxygen, the faster the fire burns. Fuel for fires includes both building contents and construction materials used for buildings. The type of construction is thus an important factor in fire control. The main types of building construction include wood frame, joisted masonry, noncombustible, masonry noncombustible, and fire-resistive.

Pre-loss fire control measures are focused on controlling heat sources and keeping them separated from fuels. Separation is also an important objective after a hostile fire breaks out. Various building design features can help prevent the spread of a hostile fire.

Fire extinguishment methods can be classified as either internal or external fire protection. Internal protection includes automatic fire detection/suppression (sprinkler) systems, portable fire extinguishers, standpipe systems, guard services, and fire brigades. External fire protection (the public fire department) offers meaningful protection only when fire hydrants are accessible and adequately supplied with water and fire department personnel are capable of responding to a fire at the facility.

Theft takes many different forms and may be committed by outsiders or by employees. Theft by outsiders includes burglary, robbery, and shoplifting. Theft by employees, also known as employee dishonesty and embezzlement, commonly presents a much more serious threat.

Various means can be used to keep burglars out of a building or at least to slow down their entry. Deadbolt locks, bars on windows, and breakage-resistant glass are examples. After a burglar gains entry into the building, safes and vaults can deny burglars access to valuable items or at least can make it harder for the burglars to gain possession of the items. Burglar alarm systems do not prevent burglars from entering, but they can deter burglars and increase the chances of apprehending them. Holdup alarms, featuring buttons or foot pedals with inconspicuous access, can alert a central station or the police that a robbery is occurring. Guards, security patrols, surveillance cameras, and various protective procedures can be used to provide further protection against burglary and robbery.

Employee theft losses are difficult to control because the dishonest employee may have access to the property, understands the employer's procedures, and may even be highly trusted by the employer. Risk control measures include accounting controls, access controls, background checks, and separation of duties.

Many explosions have the chemistry of extremely rapid combustion, and so the principles of explosion control are similar to those for the slower combustion of fires. Controlling explosions of pressure vessels (such as steam boilers) involves proper operation, maintenance, and inspection of the equipment.

Windstorm losses can be controlled through appropriate building design, the use of storm shutters and blinds, proper maintenance of roof and wall systems, and securing outdoor materials and equipment.

The best method of controlling flood and high-water losses is to avoid areas known to have flood experience. When flood exposure is unavoidable, many control measures are possible.

Where a serious earthquake exposure exists, an earthquake's effects can be reduced through building design and construction.

CHAPTER NOTE

1. The occupational fraud loss estimate was made by the Association of Certified Fraud Examiners, *2006 Report to the Nation on Occupational Fraud and Abuse*, p. 4, www.acfe.com/fraud/report/asp (accessed January 8, 2007). In contrast with the $600 billion estimate for occupational fraud losses, U.S. fire losses in 2006 were $18.1 billion, according to the Insurance Information Institute, *The III Fact Book 2008* (New York: Insurance Information Institute, 2008), p. 125.

Direct Your Learning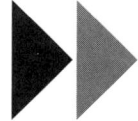

CHAPTER 2

Liability Risk Control

Educational Objectives

After learning the content of this chapter and completing the corresponding course guide assignment, you should be able to:

▶ Describe the different types of risk control techniques for commercial liability loss exposures.

▶ Explain how organizations can use general concepts of commercial liability risk control to control loss events and manage claims and potential claims.

▶ Explain how organizations can control the following loss exposures:
- Premises and operations liability
- Products liability
- Automobile liability
- Workers compensation and employers liability

OUTLINE

Risk Control Techniques

General Concepts of Commercial Liability Risk Control

Controlling Premises and Operations Liability Losses

Controlling Products Liability Losses

Controlling Automobile Liability Losses

Controlling Workers Compensation and Employers Liability Losses

Summary

Chapter 2: Develop Your Perspective

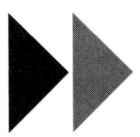

What are the main topics covered in the chapter?

This chapter describes the basic concepts involved in controlling commercial liability loss exposures, which can be categorized as controlling loss events and managing claims and potential claims. The chapter then examines specific measures for controlling common liability loss exposures.

Identify approaches that an organization can take to control loss events and manage claims that do occur.

- Why is eliminating or controlling losses preferable to managing resulting claims?
- Why might organizations have problems convincing frontline workers to participate in risk control efforts?

Why is it important to learn about these topics?

Understanding how to control commercial liability loss exposures will help you to assist customers in reducing their losses, which has benefits for your customers and for society.

Consider a small manufacturing company that has never had an organized risk control program.

- In general terms, what steps must this company take to control loss events that could otherwise result in liability losses?

How can you use what you will learn?

Evaluate a customer's commercial liability loss exposures.

- Make recommendations for improving the customer's liability risk control program.

Liability Risk Control

Risk control includes all risk management techniques intended to reduce the frequency or severity of losses. That is, risk control techniques are intended to prevent some losses from occurring or to reduce the size of losses that do occur. Risk financing techniques, in contrast, provide ways of paying for the losses that occur. A sound risk management program uses both risk control and risk financing. Risk financing is needed because losses can occur despite efforts to prevent them. Risk control is also needed because not having a loss is better than having a loss—even one whose cost is adequately financed.

An organization should consider ways of controlling its losses before it makes arrangements for financing them. By controlling losses, an organization can reduce its costs for insurance or other risk financing arrangements. In some cases, an organization may be unable to obtain insurance at any cost unless it first complies with risk control recommendations made by its insurer. Furthermore, an organization may not be able to operate legally (with or without insurance) unless it implements certain risk control measures. Worker safety measures required by the Occupational Safety and Health Act of 1970 (OSH Act) are an example.

This chapter discusses risk control techniques for controlling commercial liability loss exposures, considers general concepts of commercial liability risk control, and examines specific risk control measures that are commonly used for these commercial liability loss exposures:

- Premises and operations liability
- Products liability
- Automobile liability
- Workers compensation and employers liability

RISK CONTROL TECHNIQUES

For purposes of this discussion, a risk control measure is any specific action taken to reduce loss frequency or severity, such as installing safety devices on production machines or establishing procedures for handling medical emergencies. A risk control technique is a category of related risk control measures. Risk control techniques that can be applied to commercial liability loss exposures include the following:

- Loss prevention and loss reduction
- Avoidance
- Separation

Loss Prevention and Loss Reduction

The majority of measures taken to control commercial liability losses are either loss prevention or loss reduction, or a combination of both. **Loss prevention** is a risk control technique that reduces loss frequency (the number of occurrences in a given time period) for a particular loss exposure. For example, a manufacturer may reduce the frequency of respiratory disease among its workers by installing ventilation equipment in a work area. **Loss reduction** is a risk control technique that reduces loss severity (the monetary amount of losses that occur) for a particular loss exposure. An example of a loss reduction measure is training workers in cardiopulmonary resuscitation (CPR) and other first-aid techniques that may save the life of an accident victim.

In practice, a risk control measure may provide both loss prevention and loss reduction. For example, wearing a hard hat in a construction site may prevent injuries from occurring (thus reducing loss frequency) or lessen the severity of injuries. Similarly, obeying speed limits can reduce both the frequency and the severity of losses resulting from auto accidents.

Avoidance

Another way to control a loss exposure is to consciously choose not to assume it or to eliminate a loss exposure that already exists. This technique is called **avoidance**. If a manufacturer decides not to make a certain line of hazardous products, it avoids any losses that might have resulted from making the products. Similarly, if a motel owner fills in its swimming pool with gravel and soil, the owner will avoid liability for swimming pool accidents.

Although avoidance can be effective, it is often an unrealistic option because it can eliminate the revenue-producing assets or activities of an enterprise. In the case of a not-for-profit organization, it can eliminate assets or activities that are central to the organization's reason for existence. For example, a charity formed to provide relief to homeless persons may find that its outreach activities create some risk of bodily harm to its volunteers or employees. However, eliminating this aspect of the charity's operations might make it impossible for the charity to accomplish its goals.

Separation

Separation is a risk control technique that isolates loss exposures from one another to minimize the adverse effect of a single event. This technique is often used to control commercial property loss exposures. A common example is to separate sections of a building through the use of firewalls. With separation, the maximum possible loss at each location will be less than if all property were exposed to loss at one location. Firewalls could also reduce the building owner's liability loss exposure. If, for example, the building was an apartment building, firewalls could reduce the building owner's liability loss

Loss prevention
A risk control technique that lowers the expected frequency of loss from a particular loss exposure.

Loss reduction
A risk control technique that lowers the expected severity of losses from a particular loss exposure.

Avoidance
A risk control technique that consists of choosing not to assume a new loss exposure or eliminating a loss exposure that already exists.

Separation
A risk control technique that isolates loss exposures from one another to minimize the adverse effect of a single event.

exposure for injury to tenants because they may help prevent the spread of fire from one apartment to the next.

Apart from this example, separation does not usually lend itself to liability risk control. Although separation can effectively reduce loss exposures, it is often impractical to implement or can interfere with the organization's ability to reach its financial goals. For example, an airline could reduce its liability loss exposure for death of passengers in a single plane by using two or more small planes instead of one large plane. However, the resulting loss of efficiency in the airline's operations would preclude the use of this risk control technique.

GENERAL CONCEPTS OF COMMERCIAL LIABILITY RISK CONTROL

There are two basic approaches to controlling commercial liability losses resulting from injury to others or damage to their property:

- Controlling the events that may cause the injury or damage
- Managing liability claims (and potential claims) as soon as damage or injury has occurred or has been alleged to have occurred

To illustrate this distinction, controlling loss from liability for workers compensation benefits includes preventing on-the-job injuries and encouraging rehabilitation and early work return for employees whose injuries were not prevented. Similarly, controlling liability loss resulting from accidents involving customers in a retail store includes avoiding situations that lead to accidents and dealing effectively with each customer who appears to have been injured in an accident.

Controlling Loss Events

To control liability loss events, an organization must implement effective risk control measures as part of its overall risk management program. For an organization's risk control measures to succeed, the organization's management must be motivated to support these efforts. Once management support has been gained, an organization can develop and implement effective risk control programs.

Motivating Management

From the viewpoint of a risk management professional, effective risk control entails convincing management to pay serious attention to risk control. Managers usually are interested in activities connected to the achievement of their goals. Therefore, implementing effective risk control requires that risk management professionals understand the goals of the organization's managers.

In most organizations, financial goals are obvious. Management will tend to support risk control measures when they are presented as a means of increasing an organization's net income (through reducing expenses resulting from losses). However, the savings that result from risk control measures can only be estimated and are particularly difficult to estimate when risk control has recently been proposed or has been in place for only a short time. Nevertheless, showing the prospects for financial gain is still the most reliable way to obtain management support for risk control efforts.

Managers have other significant goals, such as following laws and regulations. For example, when the federal Occupational Safety and Health Act of 1970 was implemented, managers had to ensure that their operations met the government's standards. This type of goal is reinforced when managers can be held personally liable for losses. Managers have been fined or imprisoned for acts such as violating environmental laws and creating serious health hazards for employees.

Another goal of management is to create and preserve a good image as employer, supplier, and neighbor. Many organizations' aim for healthful working conditions is a serious organizational goal. Some organizations, such as chemical companies situated near residential areas, also want to show that they care about the health of their neighbors and therefore work hard at protecting the area's air, soil, and water from contamination. Finally, many managers have the simple humanitarian motive of not producing preventable injuries or damage to anyone.

An organization's management can show its support for risk control through a risk control policy statement that addresses these matters:

- The organization's risk control objectives
- The various activities the organization will employ to achieve those objectives
- The personnel involved in these activities and the capacity they will fulfill
- The expected performance standards
- The method used to measure compliance with these standards

The statement may help those charged with implementing risk control to secure the cooperation of other employees. Such a statement also focuses the attention of the organization's employees on specific targets for implementing and maintaining a risk control program.

Developing Risk Control Programs

The measures that an organization uses to control liability loss events should be developed as part of the organization's overall risk management program. Before risk control methods can be selected and implemented, the organization must identify and analyze the hazards that are most likely to produce significant loss. A **hazard** is any condition—such as a slippery floor or a large

Hazard
A condition that increases the frequency or severity of a loss.

volume of gasoline in storage—that increases the frequency or severity of a loss. Careful analysis of hazards is important to risk control because hazards contribute to the causes of losses. For example, in a given situation, fire might be considered the cause of a loss, but it might have been prevented by measures eliminating or lessening the hazards that increased the probability of a fire occurring.

Records of past losses can be especially helpful in identifying and analyzing present hazards. The usefulness of knowledge from past losses depends on the information derived from them. Historically, the information gathered has been too superficial. For example, when a worker had fallen off a stepladder, the traditional report was likely to note these elements:

- The unsafe act: Climbing a defective ladder
- The unsafe condition: A defective ladder
- The correction: Disposing of the defective ladder

This report overlooked crucial questions: Why was the defective ladder present? Why, given the fact that it was defective, was the ladder still in use? Dan Petersen, who posed the ladder example in his book *Techniques of Safety Management*, provides this analysis:

> To effect permanent improvement we must deal with root causes of accidents.... In our example of the defective ladder, some root causes... could be the lack of inspection procedures, the lack of management's policy, poor definition of responsibilities (supervisors didn't know they were responsible for removing the defective ladder), the lack of supervisory or employee training.[1]

An additional important matter in historical loss information concerns which events are recorded and therefore analyzed. For example, these questions might arise in connection with a manufacturer's product:

- Are customers' comments about a product that has not yet produced a serious loss recorded and analyzed to see whether they indicate that a serious loss may occur later?
- Do the comments indicate that official specifications for parts are often being exceeded and therefore suggest that quality control and inspection are likely to allow some dangerous defect to pass?
- Do the comments show a frequent particular misuse of the product that the designers did not foresee and for which they did not prepare?

For example, are "near-miss" accidents reported and investigated? A near-miss accident is an event that could have produced a serious loss but, in the particular case, did not. Examples include a dropped crane load that happens to have caused no injury and an unlocked gate to a high voltage transformer that was noticed and remedied before anyone was hurt.

Acquiring additional information involves both a cost and a benefit. In risk control, the cost is usually recognized more readily than the benefit. In general, the better organized the overall information system, the lower the cost of acquiring additional information.

In many cases, hazards with the potential for producing large liability losses can be readily identified without experiencing them and without acquiring additional information. For example, a risk manager does not have to wait for an explosion or a fire to occur to recognize that storage of a large quantity of gasoline presents the potential for a large loss. Similarly, no collapse needs to occur before the risk manager of a construction company realizes that having several employees working in an inadequately shored excavation could result in a cave-in causing loss of life. Situations such as these should get special attention even when they present no known history of losses.

Once an organization's liability hazards have been identified and analyzed, the organization must consider possible alternatives for controlling the loss exposures and select the risk control measures that are believed to be the most effective. In a very broad sense, all of these measures can be categorized as either engineering or education (human relations). That is, all the measures deal either with the nature and arrangement of things (including the work environment) or with the behavior of people.

These two means of controlling loss events are complementary. For example, an engineering approach to preventing hand injuries caused by the operation of a metal press is to equip the press with a dual hand control, a mechanism that requires the simultaneous pushing of two buttons by two hands, outside the machine. However, the press operator must be trained to operate the machine safely and efficiently. Without these complementary education measures, the engineering approach may not achieve the desired results.

Vastly different results can be achieved with any set of mechanical hazards, depending on how people behave when faced with the hazards. However, it is often easier to improve results by changing things than by changing behaviors. For example, incautious behavior of people is a major contributing factor in auto accidents.

Managing Claims and Potential Claims

Liability risk control is not restricted to actions an organization takes before accidents occur. After an accident occurs, injured persons may make liability claims against the organization. How the organization handles these liability claims can affect how much the organization ultimately must pay for the accident.

There is some conflict in the best methods for handling claims. Fraudulent or misrepresented claims are usually best resisted, whereas valid claims are usually best handled in a spirit of cooperation. In addition, many claims cannot immediately be classified as either valid or fraudulent. When a valid claim against the organization has not been successfully settled through a spirit of cooperation, the organization may need to take a more adversarial approach, especially when the claimant has hired a lawyer.

Good risk control (as well as good public, customer, and employment relations) requires ensuring that potential claimants receive prompt, effective attention to their bodily injuries or property damage. Experience has shown that prompt and cooperative attention to persons who have, or may have, suffered injury or damage for which the organization could legally be responsible reduces the number of claims filed, the frequency of attorney use, and the amounts for which claims can be settled. However, the cooperative approach does not achieve those results in cases involving fraud or significant misrepresentation. These types of claims usually require the organization to obtain legal assistance. Organizations that obtain liability insurance usually obtain claim-handling services from their insurers' claim personnel as part of the insurer's duty to investigate, settle, or defend against claims alleging injury or damage covered by the policy.

CONTROLLING PREMISES AND OPERATIONS LIABILITY LOSSES

Avoidance is sometimes feasible for handling narrowly defined aspects of an organization's premises and operations liability loss exposures. For example, a landscape contractor might decline an offer to perform certain excavation work in areas of underground piping or wiring. However, avoidance cannot be used for handling many loss exposures if the organization wants to stay in business. To deal with the many significant loss exposures that remain, an organization should seek to identify, analyze, and control hazards that could increase the frequency or severity of liability losses arising out of the organization's premises or its operations.

Addressing Hazards on the Organization's Own Premises

Many liability hazards on an organization's own premises take the form of physical conditions in buildings, structures, and grounds, often because of poor maintenance of the premises. Examples of such hazards include sidewalks in need of repair or not promptly cleared of ice and snow, defective stairways, unmarked glass door panels, poor lighting, slippery floors, and insufficient means of entering and exiting buildings. These and many other hazards can be identified, analyzed, and controlled by making frequent inspections and timely corrections.

Hazards at an organization's own premises can be eliminated or controlled, in most cases, through foresight and care. An auto repair shop, for example, may be able to reduce bodily injury claims resulting from accidents within its work areas by strictly enforcing rules that prohibit customers from entering these areas. Similarly, an organization may be able to reduce or control certain liability losses by fencing its premises.

For organizations that have customers or other members of the public entering their buildings (such as stores and public assembly places), life safety during fires is often the principal premises liability concern. Life safety engineers have developed detailed fire safety standards for particular kinds of buildings. These standards have been codified in the *Life Safety Code®* published by the National Fire Protection Association and incorporated explicitly or by reference into the building ordinances of most localities in the United States.[2]

Compliance with the applicable sections of the *Life Safety Code* is usually a legal requirement. Failure to comply is not only a breach of an ordinance (bringing fines or other penalties) but can also be substantial evidence of negligence in failing to adequately safeguard others from injury or damage by fire.

Another important risk control concern for organizations having customers or members of the public on their premises is appropriate security. An organization should exercise due care in protecting customers and other visitors from harm that may be caused by wrongdoers (for example, an intoxicated patron of a restaurant or bar, a car thief in a parking garage).

An organization might be held legally liable if a court finds that the wrongdoer's opportunity to cause injury resulted from the organization's negligence. For example, a restaurant or bar might be expected to protect its patrons against the possibility of being assaulted and battered by another patron who has become intoxicated. In this case, the appropriate risk control treatment involves training bartenders to stop serving alcohol to customers before they become intoxicated. Another important risk control measure is having personnel trained to respond to unruly patrons. Likewise, a firm that manages a shopping mall can be expected to employ a security force sufficient to patrol the mall and its parking areas, investigate suspicious behavior, and respond to emergency situations in a timely fashion.

In some business settings, such as jewelry or department stores, security efforts are focused mainly on protecting the organization's cash and merchandise against robbery or shoplifting (property loss exposures). In these cases, security personnel can become a source of liability rather than a control against it. Security guards who are improperly trained for their occupation may falsely accuse customers of shoplifting and commit unlawful acts such as assault, battery, and false arrest. Carefully hiring security personnel, checking their backgrounds, and providing them with proper training are essential to preventing liability claims that can result from their tortuous, or even criminal, acts.

Addressing Hazards Away From the Organization's Own Premises

Generally speaking, the liability losses that arise out of business operations performed away from the organization's premises are more difficult to control than those arising out of operations occurring on the insured's own premises. Many hazards on the organization's own premises are related to defective conditions that can usually be identified and corrected. In contrast, hazards away from the organization's premises can arise as work is performed and, by their nature, are often more difficult to identify and control.

For example, a manufacturing plant that is not open to the public may have minimal liability loss exposures on its own premises. But the manufacturer's operations away from these premises—such as installing its products at customers' premises—can produce a variety of costly losses, particularly because an employer is vicariously liable for its employees' negligent acts or omissions in the course of their employment.

Construction contractors, unlike firms that operate predominately from fixed locations, may be confronted with somewhat different hazards at every job site. Moreover, as construction of a building or another project progresses, the hazards at the job site change. Adding to the potential loss frequency and severity, construction work is often conducted in populated areas over which contractors have little control. For example, a contractor working in a busy metropolitan area should make sure that properly lighted barriers are installed to separate pedestrians and motorists from hazardous areas.

Operation of mobile equipment at job sites should also be the object of risk control efforts. When mobile equipment is owned by the contractor, it is the responsibility of the contractor to make sure that the equipment is maintained in safe working order and operated by employees who are properly trained. A contractor that uses backhoes or other excavating equipment should be careful to determine, before digging begins, the location of underground telephone and electrical cables and oil or natural gas pipelines.

In many cases, a contractor rents mobile equipment, sometimes with operators whose skill levels are unknown and who are not subject to the same degree of control that the contractor has over its own employees. An inexperienced crane operator who exceeds the crane's lifting capacity or fails to properly deploy outriggers can cause an accident that could result in severe bodily injury and property damage liability claims.

Addressing Contractual Liability

An organization often assumes the liability of others in contracts related to the organization's premises and operations, which can be considered part of the premises and operations liability exposure. Such contracts include leases of premises, elevator maintenance agreements, and construction contracts.

An organization can avoid contractual liability only to the extent that it refuses to be a party to these types of contracts. Such a refusal might be advisable when the organization can dictate the terms of a contract without losing valuable business to a competitor that is willing to accept the hold-harmless provision.

In other situations, it would not be advisable for the organization to risk losing a contract, especially when contractual liability insurance is available and the tax-deductible premium can either be absorbed by the organization or included in the price it charges for its products or services. This is one reason that the technique of avoiding contractual liability loss exposures is not more widely used. Another reason is that many business contracts may have been executed before the risk manager or insurance adviser becomes aware of their existence. Consequently, the contractual liability loss exposures cannot be avoided but must be insured, retained, and/or controlled.

Contractual liability loss exposures can sometimes be reduced by amending the terms of the contract involved. Whether the terms of a hold-harmless agreement can or should be amended in any given case depends on the specific situation. A complex and ambiguously worded contract may be interpreted by a court in a way that is detrimental to either party to the contract. Likewise, a loss that exceeds the scope of any contractual liability insurance can place additional burdens on both parties, particularly when the party that assumes the contract terms is financially unable to handle the defense and the settlement of any such uninsured loss.

A firm that believes a particular hold-harmless provision is too burdensome should act on it early, while the provision can still be altered, instead of reacting when the provision is enforced later. The possibility of amending the contract depends in part on the bargaining power of the parties involved. If the terms of a contract cannot be amended to more suitable conditions, the prospective indemnitor must then make a thorough assessment of the loss exposures involved to determine whether contract terms can be met if it ever becomes necessary. Of course, the potential economic profits under the contract must also be weighed against the potential costs of a loss because of the contract.

Contractual transfer works best as a risk management technique when the indemnitor is the party that is in the better position to exercise risk control measures on the loss exposures being assumed. For example, a contractor performing operations on the premises of a property owner assumes liability by contract for any claims arising in connection with the contractor's work (even though the property owner might be partly or even wholly at fault). In this situation, any measure taken to protect the contractor against direct liability (such as fencing in the work area to keep children out) may also protect the contractor against its contractual liability.

CONTROLLING PRODUCTS LIABILITY LOSSES

Virtually any organization that manufactures or sells products has a products liability loss exposure. Although products liability insurance is widely available to cover bodily injury or property damage resulting from a defective or an unsafe product, it does not cover all aspects of products liability losses.

For example, products liability insurance usually does not cover injury to the product itself or the costs of withdrawing the product from the market. It also does not cover injury to the insured's reputation (and possible loss of market share and business income) that can result from products liability suits. Moreover, a manufacturer or another seller of products may retain a sizable portion of its products liability loss exposure by way of a deductible. Finally, an organization that does not adequately control its products liability loss exposure may be unable to obtain affordable products liability insurance. For all these reasons, controlling products liability loss exposures is especially important.

In some cases, avoidance may be a viable risk control technique. For example, a pharmaceutical company may decide not to produce a new medication because of the potentially severe losses that could result from products liability claims and suits. Similarly, a sporting goods manufacturer might, because of a series of adverse court decisions, decide to stop producing football helmets. This action will not avoid liability arising out of the use of football helmets already sold, but it will avoid liability that might have resulted from future sales.

Usually, however, the goal of products liability risk control is not to avoid loss exposures but to prevent or reduce liability losses arising out of the organization's products. Manufacturers therefore take measures to ensure that their products are free from defects and reasonably safe for their intended purposes. Because these measures may not be completely effective, organizations should also establish legal defenses by documenting the actions they take to ensure that their products are safe.

Effective risk control involves every phase of the manufacturing process. Risk control measures for products liability involve all of these elements:[3]

- Design and engineering
- Manufacturing and assembly, including materials and components
- Advertising and sales literature
- Packaging
- Instruction manuals
- Installation and service operations
- Recordkeeping
- Product recall programs

Although this discussion focuses on the risk control measures of manufacturers, some measures can also apply to wholesale distributors, dealers, and retailers that package or assemble goods.

Design and Engineering

Because design and engineering are primarily devoted to planning, designing, and testing new products, they are considered to be among the more crucial functions in the manufacturing process. If a product is improperly designed or inadequately tested, controlling liability losses resulting from that product will be difficult, even though the product is manufactured and assembled according to all specifications of the design plan.

Anticipating all the possible uses and abuses to which products may be subjected is almost impossible, particularly in the case of durable goods with useful lives of many years. Designing and producing a competitively priced product that will meet future safety standards is also difficult. Consider the example of machinery sold forty or fifty years ago. Although the machinery was properly designed and manufactured by the standards of that time period, the manufacturers of those machines were later held legally accountable for injuries to machine operators because the machines did not have safety controls that are currently required.

Manufacturing and Assembly, Including Materials and Components

Following the design and testing of what a manufacturer considers to be a safe, reasonably priced, and usable product, the next crucial step in the manufacturing process involves the actual production of the product, usually with raw stock or component parts supplied by others. This is an important stage because a properly designed and tested product may still produce adverse loss exposures if it is improperly manufactured or incorrectly assembled.

These points are commonly considered to be fundamental to risk control:

- Quality control on incoming goods
- Proper storage of materials and component parts
- Quality control during the manufacturing process
- Product documentation and recordkeeping
- Full testing before shipment
- Proper marking of products or containers

It is important to properly handle, inspect, and test both raw materials, obtained from suppliers, that are transformed into a finished product and component parts supplied by other manufacturers that are assembled as part of the finished product. Exposures to loss from materials and components confront many manufacturers because many do not produce a product in its entirety. Such manufacturers should be just as careful in handling these components as they are in handling products or parts of their own manufacture.

Advertising and Sales Literature

An organization whose product is properly planned, designed, tested, manufactured, and assembled can still face significant liability loss exposures when its advertising or sales literature is misleading or lacks sufficient warnings or instructions. Consequently, advertising and sales literature should be reviewed and approved by engineering staff, legal staff, and the products safety committee to ensure that all materials accurately represent the use and capabilities of the product.

Manufacturers must also be careful not to make statements that are exaggerated or untrue. For example, costly liability losses have all but eliminated the practice of manufacturers describing their products as "safe" or "foolproof."

Many products, particularly durable goods, cannot be designed and produced to withstand all possible abuses, nor can they be built to operate without certain special precautions. Advertising and sales literature should therefore communicate precisely what products can and cannot do and what must be done to operate or use them safely.

Packaging

Packaging is essential to the distribution of nearly all products and includes containers for toxic chemicals, explosives, and heavy machinery. From a legal perspective, packaging is considered to be a product itself. If a package is defective or not suitable for its intended purpose, the manufacturer or seller of the package can be held legally liable for injury or damage resulting from the package's failure. Therefore, the design and production of packaging is just as important as the design and production of any other product.

Instruction Manuals

Manufacturers often publish manuals containing detailed instructions on how to install, operate, maintain, service, and repair their products. Several basic points should be considered in preparing instruction manuals:

- What may appear clear to the writer of the manual may not necessarily be clearly understood by others. Terminology and language, therefore, should be used with the end user in mind.
- The manual should reference specific standards and codes that govern the installation and operation of the product.
- Instructions should emphasize the critical and/or procedural steps that are important for properly operating the product and for minimizing operation failures.
- Appropriate warnings may be included as necessary, such as for flammable or hazardous products.
- Pictures and photos may be necessary to illustrate certain aspects of the product, such as a machine with proper guards in place or a piece of equipment requiring an operator to wear protective gear for safe operation.

Installation and Service Operations

After a product has been sold to a consumer, either independent service organizations or the manufacturer itself may provide installation, maintenance, and repair services. If performed properly, service operations can be viewed as products liability risk control because proper service can identify and remedy problems in the product before breakdown or injury occurs. Because service personnel usually are the first to know that a product is not functioning properly, they should be the first to notify the manufacturer. Early identification of product difficulties will not only control the size of problems but will also reduce the expenses that usually accompany them. Training of service personnel, appropriate technical support, and a direct line of communication between service personnel and the manufacturer are therefore important aspects of products liability risk control.

Recordkeeping

Maintaining records is a key element of products liability risk control. Organizations are subject to a variety of federal laws that require them to keep certain records of their products. These laws include, but are not limited to, the Consumer Product Safety Act; the Federal Food, Drug and Cosmetic Act; the Poison Prevention Packaging Act; and the Child Protection and Toy Act. Every organization that is subject to these or similar laws needs to understand and comply with the applicable recordkeeping requirements.

To be effective in supporting risk control efforts, records should be kept on all materials that go into the product, including the components of others, and on the quality control standards of the entire manufacturing process—from research, design, and testing to sales and service. These records should be maintained for at least the anticipated life of the product. When the product's life cannot be anticipated, an organization should maintain the records indefinitely.

In addition to complying with legal requirements, records are essential in any risk control program for at least three reasons:

- Records can be used in locating the source of the problem that causes the production of poor quality products that have to be rejected or recalled. For example, records may show that the component of a supplier was not properly tested before being used, or that proper quality control standards were not maintained as required during the production process. Without records, it may be impossible, or possible only at considerable expense, to determine problem areas.
- Records can facilitate the systematic withdrawal of products from the market or from use when they are known to be or suspected of being defective or unreasonably dangerous.
- Records also can aid organizations in defending against lawsuits. In the majority of cases, manufacturers do not learn about their products liability losses until they are sued. When this happens, manufacturers must move quickly to produce detailed records that will enable their attorneys to prepare their cases. The more comprehensive the records, the easier it is for manufacturers to support their arguments. Many manufacturers have won cases with records by illustrating that it was not their product that caused injury or damage but negligence of the user.

Three types of documentation have proved to be especially important in products litigation: performance documents, audit manuals, and genealogy tracing documents.

Performance documents include these:

- In-house guideline documents such as a drafting standards manual, a safety code manual, and a manual of engineering test procedures
- Checklists used in design, construction, testing, inspection, or warnings
- External relations documents such as suppliers' manuals and customer relations manuals

Audit manuals relate to monitoring whether the organization is meeting the requirements stated in the performance documents, including the use of checklists. Important audits are those conducted by the board of directors and staff groups. External certifications by private testing groups, consumer associations, accreditation agencies, and government regulators are also important.

Genealogy tracing documents include all records that enable the organization to trace the life history of the product by serial and model numbers or by batch and production-run numbers.

Product Recall Programs

When a product proves to be defective or dangerous in actual use or, in some cases, only is suspected of being dangerous, the Consumer Product Safety Commission (a federal agency) may require the manufacturer of the product to recall or withdraw the product. The manufacturer may also be required to notify consumers to bring the product to an authorized agent of the manufacturer for inspection, adjustment, or repair. Even if governmental authorities do not require a recall, a manufacturer may voluntarily withdraw a product from the market if it suspects that its product is defective or dangerous. Recalling products can be an effective risk control measure because the recall enables the manufacturer to correct problems before people get hurt or property is damaged.

Accordingly, a logical part of a products liability risk control program is an organized system for communicating with consumers and, if necessary, recalling products from the market or from use. This system must be structured so that notice of a defective or an unreasonably unsafe product can be given as promptly as possible to distributors, retailers, and consumers. The system must also be organized to facilitate the prompt withdrawal, inspection, repair, or replacement of products that are known to be or suspected of being harmful. Because speed is essential in recalling products, an organization should have a recall program that can be implemented the moment the need arises.

Recordkeeping is an essential part of any product recall program. Records can help identify the particular batch or serialized group of products that need to be recalled, repaired, or replaced, as well as the distributors and the geographic areas of sale. As a product is designed, produced, tested, coded, and shipped, records should be made and retained at all stages.

Organizing and maintaining an effective product recall program can be expensive. However, if such a program is not implemented, the repercussions can be severe. The whole purpose of a risk control program can be defeated if measures are not taken to prevent or reduce losses from exposures known to exist. Consumers can also lose confidence in a company that does not seem to care about the welfare of those who have bought its products. If a product falls within the jurisdiction of the Consumer Product Safety Act, a company also faces serious penalties for any failure to comply with the Consumer Product Safety Commission's requirements dealing with communicating product defects and product withdrawals to consumers.

CONTROLLING AUTOMOBILE LIABILITY LOSSES

Poorly maintained vehicles, severe weather conditions, road conditions, faults of other motorists, and many other factors can all contribute to an organization's adverse loss experience with autos. However, auto accidents are largely attributable to the human element, that is, to drivers' psychological and physical attributes (habits, skills, temperament, vision, reflexes, and so forth). Therefore, for purposes of identifying principal sources of auto liability exposures, the organization that maintains records on the frequency and severity of its past losses is at an advantage because it may be able to identify losses likely to recur and employees likely to become involved in future accidents.

Automobile liability risk control measures are primarily concerned with selecting, training, and supervising drivers. Additional risk control measures involve acquisition of safe vehicles, vehicle maintenance, and proper scheduling and routing.

Selecting, Training, and Supervising Drivers

An organization should screen prospective employee-drivers from the standpoint of their driving experience, as well as their past loss experience and moving traffic convictions. A record of one or more driving under the influence (DUI) or driving while intoxicated (DWI) convictions may be sufficient grounds for an employer to reject a prospective employee-driver. Motor vehicle reports (MVRs), which show drivers' records of traffic violations and license suspensions, can usually be obtained from the state licensing authority and are another source of information.

Periodically obtaining MVRs on current employees is another prudent measure. A driver who had a clean record when hired and has had no on-the-job auto accidents may nevertheless have had several auto accidents while not working. These accidents may indicate the need for corrective measures. Some employers also require current (and prospective) employee-drivers to undergo drug and alcohol testing.

When appropriate measures are taken to identify sources of auto accidents and moving violations, the management of an organization can then determine actions that will prevent or reduce auto liability losses. If any drivers have had a series of traffic violations or accidents, or both, the best course may be to replace those drivers. In many companies, a single DUI/DWI offense may be reason for dismissing a driver. For drivers who have had few traffic violations and one or two minor accidents, the best course may be to require the drivers to attend driver safety classes. An organization may even choose to require all of its drivers to attend driver safety classes as a preventive measure. If an organization does not take corrective measures with problem drivers and does not monitor its program on a periodic basis to see whether adjustments are necessary, its entire auto risk control program may be in vain.

Organizations should also formulate and enforce standard safe operating procedures for any employee who is in any way involved with motor vehicles. For example, material handlers who load and unload motor vehicles, as well as mechanics who maintain vehicles, are just as important to a company's risk control program as its drivers. Moreover, the organization should also consider these persons as drivers:

- Employees who drive rental autos while conducting the organization's business
- Employees who drive their own autos while conducting the organization's business
- Employees' family members who are permitted to operate autos owned by the organization

Although an employer cannot apply the same driver controls on employees' family members as it applies to its employees, it can place some basic guidelines on use of company cars by nonemployees. For example, it could have a policy of not allowing family members under a certain age to drive company cars under any circumstances.

Other Measures for Controlling Automobile Liability Losses

Other measures for controlling auto loss exposures include the acquisition of safe vehicles, proper maintenance of vehicles, and proper routing and scheduling.

What constitutes a safe vehicle can vary, depending on the services that the organization performs with its vehicles. A pickup truck that is a safe vehicle for transporting light tools and supplies would be unsafe for transporting items weighing more than the vehicle's load capacity. Thus, a vehicle acquired to perform a type of work must be safe for the anticipated work. In the case of passenger vehicles, crash test results and research reports from the Insurance Institute for Highway Safety can be helpful in selecting safe vehicles.

To ensure proper maintenance of vehicles, a designated person in the organization should be responsible for keeping a preventive maintenance schedule for each vehicle and making sure that all vehicles receive their scheduled maintenance on time. The same person should keep records of the maintenance and repairs performed on each vehicle.

Proper routing of vehicles can be helpful not only in reducing driving times but in helping drivers to avoid congested areas or poor roads that could increase the frequency of accidents. Likewise, proper scheduling of drivers can help prevent accidents resulting from an overly demanding schedule that requires operators to drive too fast or for too long.

CONTROLLING WORKERS COMPENSATION AND EMPLOYERS LIABILITY LOSSES

Many organizations dedicate more of their resources to controlling workers compensation and employers liability losses than they do to controlling any other liability losses. These are some of the reasons for this priority:

- State and federal laws require certain risk control activities.
- Claim frequency is higher for workers compensation and employers liability losses than for most other losses.
- Risk control measures are highly effective in preventing or reducing these losses.
- Employers have a strong incentive for controlling workers compensation losses, either because they self-insure some or all of the loss exposure or because their workers compensation insurance rates are directly affected by their loss history through experience rating or retrospective rating.
- For humanitarian reasons and good employee relations, employers wish to prevent these losses from occurring.

The costs of providing workers compensation benefits are only part of the losses employers sustain because of an occupational injury. In addition to the cost of workers compensation benefits, these may be among the consequences of a workplace accident:

- Time lost by other employees who stop work to assist the injured employee or for other reasons
- Time lost by supervisors while assisting the employee, investigating the accident, securing a replacement, and filling out forms and answering questions
- Damage to machines or spoilage of material

Depending on many factors, these incidental or hidden costs can exceed the cost of the actual workers compensation benefits.[4] Recognition of these additional costs and the fact that most such costs are uninsurable emphasizes the importance of risk control for managing workers compensation and employers liability loss exposures.

Applying risk control to workers compensation and employers liability loss exposures, particularly in industrial settings, can be a complex task that requires the services of safety professionals, industrial hygienists, and other specialists. Although some large organizations employ in-house risk control professionals, most employers obtain risk control services either from their insurer's risk control personnel or from outside contractors.

These are three important aspects of controlling workers compensation and employers liability losses:

- Loss and hazard analysis
- Major categories of risk control measures
- Occupational Safety and Health Act compliance

Loss and Hazard Analysis

Loss and hazard analysis is a crucial first step in controlling workers compensation and employers liability losses. The objective of loss and hazard analysis is to analyze the losses actually experienced by the organization and the hazards leading to these losses that might lead to future losses.

The analyst studies losses that have occurred in the past and the activities that were the sources of those losses. The analyst measures the loss frequency and loss severity and the predictability of the loss experience. To support such analysis, organizations must keep records that provide this information and permit comparisons with the experience of other organizations.

The analysis of accidents for worker safety purposes requires detailed information and comparisons. For example, the analyst must know these facts to determine the causes of an accident:

- Who was involved
- What specific operation was being performed
- When the accident occurred
- The department or section in which the accident occurred
- How the employee was injured
- Whether the employee was committing an unsafe act before the accident occurred and, if so, whether the unsafe act was the fault of the employee or management
- Whether defective tools, equipment, materials, and facilities contributed to the accident
- Whether environmental factors such as noise, temperature extremes, or poor illumination were present

Accident investigation forms for employee injuries should be designed to provide as much of this information as possible but still be relatively easy to understand and not too burdensome to complete. These forms are almost always completed by supervisors or subordinates who are close to the scene of the accident but who may see little value in the report itself. An employee who is experienced in completing an accident investigation report should be available to assist supervisors or subordinates who are unfamiliar with conducting accident investigations or who do not understand why they are important.

Computers and common software programs can be extremely useful in analyzing the data gathered through these forms. This information alerts the analyst to what caused these accidents and how they might be prevented in the future. The information also provides a base for allocating loss costs among departments or plants, which can be used to provide financial or other incentives for risk control.

Many hazards may exist that have not yet resulted in any accidents. To identify these hazards, the analyst must use some of the methods commonly used for identifying loss exposures: inspection of the premises and activities; interviews with employees; questionnaires; and study of the legal, social, and economic environment—particularly changes in workers compensation laws and their interpretation. The information gathered may also be useful in estimating the probable frequency and severity of future losses.

Various system safety approaches have been developed to further analyze the hazards revealed by the accident data or separate hazard identification. **System safety** is a safety engineering technique that considers the mutual effects of the interrelated elements of a system on one another throughout the system's life cycle. Some representative system safety analysis techniques are summarized in Exhibit 2-1.

> **System safety**
> A safety engineering technique that considers the mutual effects of the interrelated elements of a system on one another throughout the system's life cycle.

Major Categories of Risk Control Measures

After identifying and analyzing the hazards facing its employees, an employer must examine, select, implement, and monitor appropriate risk control measures that will lower the frequency and severity of workers compensation and employers liability losses. The selection of risk control measures depends largely on the applicable hazards, which can vary greatly by the business or industry in which the employer is engaged. The measures used to control occupational injuries can be classified into these broad categories:

- Designing (or redesigning) buildings, equipment, or work processes for safety
- Screening, training, and supervising employees
- Managing claims, including rehabilitation

EXHIBIT 2-1

Summary of System Safety Analysis Techniques

Technique	How the Technique Is Applied
Job safety analysis	Analyze a repetitive task (usually in a person/machine industrial context) to determine potential hazards if each action is not performed.
Scenario analysis	Brainstorm conceivable severe accidents, trace their possible causes and consequences, and identify feasible preventive measures.
Cost/benefit analysis	Assign dollar (or other measurable) values to the costs and benefits expected from proposed changes in a system and select the change(s) promising the greatest benefit over cost.
Program evaluation and review technique (PERT)	Develop a network of sequenced, time-critical events essential to the success of a project so that these events can be scheduled to ensure timely project completion.
Fault tree analysis	Identify a negative result of system performance and trace every failure of a system component back through a logic tree that can produce this negative result.
Failure mode and effect analysis	Identify conceivable failures of each system component and, through a logic tree, project the effects of these failures on system performance.
Technique of human error rate prediction	Break down human activity into specific tasks, determine the probabilities of specific errors while performing each task, and compute the overall probability of some error during that activity.

Adapted with permission from P. L. Clemens, "A Compendium of Hazard Identification and Evaluation Techniques for System Safety Applications," *Hazard Prevention*, March/April 1982, pp. 11-18.

Designing for Safety

Workplace safety can be achieved through the design (or redesign) of buildings, equipment, and work processes—a goal that is referred to as "safety through design."

> Safety through design is defined as the integration of hazard analysis and risk assessment methods early in the design and engineering stages and the taking of the actions necessary so that the risks of injury or damage are at an acceptable level.[5]

Safety experts recommend that employers apply these priorities when designing for safety:

- First priority—Eliminate hazards. An employer should always eliminate any hazards that can be eliminated. For example, a processing company might be able to substitute a safe solvent for one that can cause cancer. By replacing the carcinogenic solvent with the safe one, the employer eliminates a hazard.

- Second priority—Reduce hazards to acceptable levels. If certain hazards cannot be eliminated, the employer should reduce them to acceptable levels through the use of safety design features or devices, such as a guard that keeps a machine operator's hands out of a dangerous part of a machine.
- Third priority—Develop systems to detect hazards and warn workers. If certain hazards cannot be eliminated or reduced through safety design features, the employer should develop systems to detect hazardous conditions and warn workers of the conditions. For example, a chemical company may be unwilling to stop producing a particular chemical and therefore unable to eliminate (or reduce to an acceptable level) the workplace hazard posed by this chemical. The possibility remains that a quantity of the chemical sufficient to injure employees could leak into the plant's atmosphere. Accordingly, the company could install a detection and warning system that would alert employees before they were exposed to dangerous levels of the chemical. This would enable employees to take appropriate action before dangerous levels of the chemical accumulated.
- Fourth priority—Develop safe operating procedures and provide safety training. If it is impossible or impractical to eliminate hazards, reduce them to acceptable levels, or develop detection and warning systems, an employer can develop and implement safe operating procedures and provide safety training programs for its employees. For example, the hazards of using ladders at work sites cannot be eliminated or reduced to acceptable levels through safe design alone. Detection and warning systems are also ineffective. However, training employees to use ladders safely would be an effective approach to preventing injuries.
- Fifth priority—Use personal protective equipment. If all other techniques are ineffective, using personal protective equipment can help prevent occupational injury. Examples of personal protective equipment are hard hats, respirators, gloves, safety glasses, earplugs, lifelines, and safety nets.

Employers often use two or more of these design priorities to address the same causes of occupational injury. For example, a potential cause of occupational injury is fire, and many fire hazards can increase the frequency or severity of injury. An employer can perhaps eliminate some fire hazards or reduce them to acceptable levels. To address other fire hazards, the employer's building can be designed (or redesigned) with various fire controls, such as a fire detection and suppression system, fire extinguishers, and firewalls. (In many cases, an ordinance or building code will require those controls.) In addition, the employer can develop fire safety programs to train employees in preventing fires and, if a fire occurs, in fighting fires and evacuating the building.

Ergonomics
A human-centered discipline that focuses on ways to fit work to the worker.

An important element of achieving safety through design is **ergonomics**, also called human factors engineering.

> Ergonomics deals with the realization and application of worker needs, abilities, limitations, and characteristics to the design of machines, tools, jobs, and workplaces that can result in productive, safe, comfortable, and efficient use. That is, ergonomics is a human-centered discipline that focuses on ways to fit the work to the worker.[6]

Ergonomics addresses the environmental problems causing work-related musculoskeletal disorders (WMSDs), which each year account for more than $15 to $20 billion in workers compensation costs. Common examples of WMSDs are carpal tunnel syndrome, epicondylitis (tennis elbow), tendonitis, bursitis, and lower back pain. Many organizations have implemented formal ergonomics programs as a way to integrate ergonomics into their overall process of designing for safety. These are the key components of an ergonomics program:

- Management commitment and support of ergonomics activities
- Management of injury cases to ensure that WMSDs are promptly identified and effectively treated
- Training and education of all employees involved
- Incorporation of a workplace improvement process into the design stage of new buildings, equipment, and work processes

The number of different risk control measures that employers may implement in the process of designing for safety is immense. Appropriate risk control measures can differ dramatically by the particular business or industry in which an organization is engaged. The risk control measures implemented in a coal mine are quite different from those implemented in an office building, a factory, or a construction site. The following list of general areas of risk control focus provides a sense of the range of measures possible:

- Buildings and facility layout
- Maintenance of facilities
- Boilers and unfired pressure vessels
- Safeguarding of tools and production machinery
- Personal protective equipment
- Industrial sanitation
- Electrical safety
- Fire protection
- Materials handling and storage
- Hoisting and conveying equipment
- Mobile equipment
- Hand and portable power tools
- Woodworking machinery
- Welding and cutting
- Metalworking machinery

Screening, Training, and Supervising Employees

A second major category of measures for controlling workers compensation and employers liability losses is proper screening, training, and supervision of employees. Such measures can reduce the incidence of unsafe practices that can cause accidents injuring the unsafe employee or other employees.

In hiring employees and assigning them to a job, the organization should consider not only their ability to do the job, but also their ability to do it in a way that will not result in injuries to themselves or to their fellow employees. Thorough investigation of prospective employees might reveal a history of substance abuse, fraudulent filing of workers compensation claims, or malingering after occupational injuries. Having accurate background information on an applicant allows the employer to select employees that do not pose an unacceptable risk of causing injury to themselves or others, or possibly even filing fraudulent workers compensation claims or exaggerating the disability resulting from an actual injury.

New employees need to be properly trained in safe job procedures. This type of training is particularly important for employees who operate power tools or equipment or are otherwise exposed to workplace hazards. After the initial training, employees' awareness of safety issues can be maintained through additional training sessions, employee meetings, newsletters, and memos.

In its *Accident Prevention Manual for Industrial Operations: Administration and Programs*, the National Safety Council illustrates the importance of proper training and supervision.[7] The Council cites four examples of unsafe practices that can result from employees' deviating from standard job procedures:

- Using equipment without authority
- Operating equipment at an unsafe speed or in any other improper way
- Removing safety devices or rendering them inoperative
- Using defective tools

Some of the possible explanations of why these unsafe practices occurred and how they might be avoided include the following:

Explanation	Countermeasure
No known standard for safe job procedure exists	Develop such a procedure and include in training
Employee did not know the standard job procedure	Train the employee in the correct procedure
Employee knew the procedure but did not follow it	Consider an employee performance evaluation; test validity of the procedure
Employee knew the procedure but did not follow it because of work pressures or supervisor's influence	Consider changes in work pressures; counsel worker and supervisor

Supervisors who are responsible for job safety should be selected and trained with this responsibility in mind. The purpose of the training is to emphasize the continuing importance of job safety and to provide the supervisors with the technical and human relations knowledge they need to be effective.

Managing Claims, Including Rehabilitation

After an accident occurs or an employee is diagnosed with an occupational disease, the organization's objective should be to minimize the severity of the loss to the worker and the organization. How the worker's claim is managed can greatly influence the final outcome.

The organization should have a plan that assigns responsibility to someone within the organization to implement a plan that becomes effective following an injury. The plan should include procedures for providing emergency care, communicating with the injured employee's supervisors and fellow workers, and investigating the accident. While the employee is undergoing medical treatment and subsequent convalescence, the plan should provide for transportation of the injured employee to proper medical facilities. If the employer demonstrates at an early stage sincere concern for the welfare of the employee, the employee is much less likely to seek the help of an attorney, which can increase the magnitude of the loss.

The workers compensation system eliminates the need for most employees to sue their employers in order to establish the employer's obligation to provide benefits for work-related injuries. Nevertheless, injured employees may sue their employers or their employers' insurers to receive greater benefits than they have been awarded. For example, an employee who has been awarded benefits for a temporary disability may sue to receive benefits for a permanent disability.

At the appropriate time, the worker should receive physical and vocational rehabilitation and be encouraged to return to active employment, preferably with the same employer. The organization should have a return-to-work program that includes light-duty assignments, part-time schedules, and job modifications.

Occupational Safety and Health Act Compliance

As part of their risk control activities for workers compensation and employers liability losses, employers must comply with the safety and health standards issued by the Secretary of Labor or approved state plans under the federal Occupational Safety and Health Act of 1970 (OSH Act). The OSH Act is applicable to all employers with one or more employees engaged in a business. Specifically excluded from the OSH Act are all federal, state, and local government employees and some employers, such as coal mine operators, subject to separate safety laws.

Standards of the OSH Act incorporate by reference many standards developed by private organizations such as the American Society for Testing and Materials, the Society of Automotive Engineers, and Underwriters Laboratories. Federal officers check compliance with the OSH Act's standards by making periodic inspections of selected businesses. Unless the employer demands a search warrant, the officers can enter the premises at any time. Employers seldom demand a warrant because this demand usually delays the inspection only a day or two. The OSH Act has assigned most of the inspection time to high-priority cases: accidents that have resulted in fatalities or in the hospitalization of several employees, employee complaints alleging imminent danger, high-hazard industries, and establishments cited previously for serious violations.

If the inspection reveals violation of a specific standard or the general duty to provide a safe workplace, the officer may issue a written citation that the employer must display at or near the place where the alleged violation occurred. Citations for serious violations are accompanied by a fine. Citations for lesser violations may or may not result in a fine. In either case, the employer must correct the penalty by a specified date. Failure to correct an uncontested violation by that date may result in a fine for each day that the violation is not corrected. In case of willful or repeated violations, the OSH Act may impose sizable fines. An employer who willfully violates a standard that causes the death of an employee may face criminal penalties as well.

SUMMARY

The purpose of risk control is to prevent losses from occurring or to reduce the severity of those losses that do occur. A sound risk management program includes risk control in addition to insurance or other risk financing techniques.

Techniques used to control commercial liability losses include loss prevention and loss reduction, avoidance, and separation. Avoidance and separation are often impractical for controlling commercial liability losses and therefore have only limited use.

Two basic aspects of controlling liability losses are controlling loss events and managing of liability claims.

Efficient risk control will not occur within an organization unless the organization's management is motivated to support risk control efforts. Showing that risk control promotes financial gain is the most reliable way to motivate management. However, management may also be motivated by a desire to operate legally, to create and preserve a good image, or, for humanitarian reasons, to avoid harming others. Once management has been motivated to support risk control activities, an organization can develop and implement effective risk control programs.

The process for selecting and implementing risk control measures parallels the risk management process. An organization must first identify and analyze the hazards that are most likely to produce significant loss. If analyzed properly, records of past losses are helpful in identifying and analyzing present hazards.

Once an organization's liability hazards have been identified and analyzed, the organization must consider the possible alternatives and select the risk control measures that are believed to be the most effective. All the means of controlling loss events can be categorized as either engineering or education. Achieving an appropriate balance between the two is an important part of liability risk control.

After a loss event has occurred, prompt action (such as first aid) can minimize damages even if the organization is legally liable. Ethical and humane treatment of injured persons can help to avoid liability claims or mitigate the damages that must be paid.

The premises and operations liability exposure consists of hazards on an organization's own premises and hazards arising out of the organization's operations at other locations. Liability hazards on an organization's own premises include physical conditions in buildings, structures, and grounds, often due to poor maintenance. These hazards can be found and controlled by making frequent inspections and timely corrections.

More difficult for organizations to control, generally speaking, are liability losses arising out of operations performed away from the organization's own premises. Contractual liability exposures that are considered part of the premises and operations liability loss exposure can sometimes be reduced by amending the terms of the contract(s) involved.

Products liability risk control measures should form an integral part of the manufacturing process and involve each of these elements:

- Design and engineering
- Manufacturing and assembly, including materials and components
- Advertising and sales literature
- Packaging
- Instruction manuals
- Installation and service operations
- Recordkeeping
- Product recall programs

Although many factors can contribute to automobile liability losses, most auto accidents result from human error. Consequently, many automobile liability risk control measures focus on human factors. The driving records of new and existing employee-drivers should be carefully reviewed and monitored. Corrective action, ranging from requiring driver safety courses to dismissing unsafe drivers, should be taken when appropriate. Acquisition of safe vehicles, proper maintenance, and proper routing and scheduling are also important.

Workers compensation and employers liability losses are important to control because workers compensation benefits are only part of the costs associated with on-the-job accidents. Risk control can reduce both workers compensation benefit payments as well as the hidden costs resulting from job-related accidents. Loss and hazard analysis is a crucial first step in controlling workers compensation and employers liability losses. The objective of loss and hazard analysis is to analyze the losses actually experienced by the organization and the hazards leading to these losses that might lead to future losses.

After analyzing the hazards facing its employees, an employer must select, implement, and monitor appropriate risk control measures. The selection of risk control measures can vary greatly by the business or industry in which the employer is engaged. The measures used to control occupational injuries can be classified into the following broad categories:

- Designing (or redesigning) buildings, equipment, or work processes for safety
- Screening, training, and supervising employees
- Managing claims, including rehabilitation and early return-to-work programs

Compliance with the Occupational Safety and Health Act of 1970 is another important risk control activity because failure to comply can result in fines against the organization or even imprisonment of its managers.

CHAPTER NOTES

1. This analysis and quotation come from Dan Petersen, *Techniques of Safety Management* (New York: McGraw-Hill Book Company, 1971), pp. 13–15.
2. *Life Safety Code®* is a registered trademark of the National Fire Protection Association, Quincy, MA 02169.
3. For a more in-depth treatment of products liability risk control measures, see the National Safety Council's *Product Safety Management Guidelines*, 2nd ed. (Itasca, Ill.: National Safety Council, 1997).
4. Herbert W. Heinrich, *Industrial Accident Prevention*, 4th ed. (New York: McGraw-Hill Book Co., 1959), pp. 50–52. The concept of hidden workers compensation costs was first advanced by Herbert W. Heinrich. For the cases he studied, Heinrich found that the hidden costs were four times the workers compensation benefit costs. Subsequent writers have suggested that the four-to-one ratio is too high or varies with the type of case. All these sources agree, however, that workers compensation benefits are only part of the costs associated with occupational injuries.
5. This quotation, as well as the information presented about designing for safety, is from Chapter 1, "Safety Through Design," in *Accident Prevention Manual for Business and Industry: Engineering & Technology*, 12th ed. (Itasca, Ill.: National Safety Council, 2001), p. 4.
6. This quotation, as well as the information presented about ergonomics, is from Chapter 16, "Ergonomics Program," in *Accident Prevention Manual for Business & Industry: Administration & Programs*, 12th ed. (Itasca, Ill.: National Safety Council, 2001), p. 390.
7. *Accident Prevention Manual for Business & Industry: Administration & Programs*, p. 110.

Index

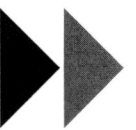

Page numbers in boldface refer to definitions of Key Words and Phrases.

A

Access control, **1.38**
Accounting control, **1.38**
Advertising and sales literature, 2.14
Alarm systems, 1.35
Area protection (space protection), **1.35**
Arson, preventing, 1.20
Autoignition temperature, **1.8**
Avoidance, **2.4**

B

Background checks, 1.40
Building construction, types of, 1.10–1.15

C

Carbon dioxide system, **1.25**
Central station system, **1.28**
Claims and potential claims, managing, 2.8
Claims, rehabilitation, managing, 2.27
Commercial liability
    addressing, 2.11
    risk control, general concepts, 2.5
Construction
    building, types of, 1.10–1.15
    fire-resistive, 1.15
    frame, 1.10
    heavy timber, 1.13
    joisted masonry, 1.10
    masonry noncombustible, 1.14
    modified fire-resistive, 1.15
    noncombustible, 1.13

D

Deluge system, **1.23**
Designing for safety, 2.23
Detection and signaling systems, 1.27
Drivers, selecting, training, and supervision of, 2.18
Dry chemical system, **1.24**
Dry-pipe system, **1.23**
Duties, separation of, 1.40

E

Earthquake, 1.43
Employees, screening, training, and supervision of, 2.25
Ergonomics, **2.24**
Explosion, 1.40

F

Fire brigades, 1.30
Fire control measures, pre-loss, 1.15–1.21
Fire detection/suppression systems, automatic, 1.21–1.22
Fire division, **1.19**
Fire, elements of, 1.6–1.10
Fire extinguishers, 1.28
    types of, 1.29
Fire extinguishment methods, 1.21–1.32
Fire load, **1.9**
Fire protection, external, 1.30
Fire-resistive construction, **1.15**
Fire spread, limiting
    horizontal, 1.18
    vertical, 1.17
Fire stops, **1.18**
Fire wall, **1.19**
Flash point, **1.8**
Flood, 1.42
Frame construction, 1.10
Fuel, 1.8

G

Guard services, 1.29
Guards or security patrols, 1.37

H

Halon (and similar) systems, 1.26
Halon, **1.26**
Hazard, **2.6**
Hazards
    away from organization's premises, addressing, 2.10
    on organization's premises, addressing, 2.9
Heat, 1.6

Heat sources,
    controlling, 1.15
        separating, from fuels, 1.16
Heavy timber construction (mill construction), 1.13
Holdup alarm, **1.36**

I

Installation and service operations, 2.15

J

Joisted masonry construction, **1.10**

L

Liability losses, controlling
    automobile, 2.18–2.20
    premises and operations, 2.9–2.12
    products liability, 2.12–2.16
    workers compensation and employers liability, 2.20–2.28
Life safety in fires, 1.32
Local system, **1.27**
Loss and hazard analysis, 2.21
Loss events, controlling, 2.5
Loss prevention, **2.4**
Loss reduction, **2.4**

M

Management, motivating, 2.5
Manufacturing and assembly, 2.14
Masonry noncombustible construction, **1.14**
Materials and components, 2.14
Modified fire-resistive construction, **1.15**

N

Noncombustible construction, **1.13**
Noncombustibles, substitution of for combustibles, 1.20

O

Object protection, **1.36**
Occupational Safety and Health Act, compliance with, 2.27
Oxygen, 1.7

P

Packaging, 2.15
Perimeter system, **1.35**
Preaction system, **1.23**

Premises and operations liability losses, controlling, 2.9–2.12
Product recall programs, 2.17
Products liability losses, controlling, 2.12–2.16
Proprietary system, **1.28**
Protective procedures, 1.37

R

Remote station system, **1.28**
Risk control
    for burglary and robbery losses, 1.34–1.37
    commercial liability, general concepts, 2.5–2.9
    for employee theft losses, 1.38–1.40
    for fire losses, 1.5–1.33
    for other causes of loss, 1.40–1.43
    for theft losses, 1.33–1.40
Risk control measures, major categories of, 2.22
Risk control programs, developing, 2.6
Risk control techniques, 2.3–2.5

S

Separation, **2.4**
Standpipe system, **1.29**
Supervised system, **1.37**
Suppression systems, automatic, 1.22
Surveillance cameras, 1.37
System safety, **2.22**
    analysis techniques, summary of, 2.23

T

Theft prevention system, internal, 1.39

W

Water damage, controlling, 1.31
Workers compensation and employers liability losses, controlling, 2.20–2.28
Water spray system, **1.23**
Water systems, 1.22
Wet chemical systems, 1.24
Wet-pipe system, **1.23**
Windstorm, 1.41